Extending the Runway
Leadership Strategies for Venture Capitalists and Executives of Funded Companies

Dave Berkus

Mat #40687628

BOOK & ARTICLE IDEA SUBMISSIONS

If you are a C-Level executive, senior lawyer, or venture capitalist interested in submitting a book or article idea to the Aspatore editorial board for review, please email 011.Aspatore.Authors@thomson.com. Aspatore is especially looking for highly specific ideas that would have a direct financial impact on behalf of a reader. Completed publications can range from 2 to 2,000 pages. Include your book/article idea, biography, and any additional pertinent information.

WRITING & EDITORIAL ASSISTANCE

In select instances Aspatore will assist in helping our authors generate the content for their publication via phone interviews. Aspatore editors create interview questions that help generate the main content for the book or article. The content from the phone interviews is then transcribed and edited for review and enhancement by the author. If this method could be of assistance in helping you find the time to write an article or book, please email 111.Aspatore.Editorial@thomson.com for more information, along with your biography and your publication idea.

©2006 Thomson/Aspatore
All rights reserved. Printed in the United States of America.

Managing Editor, Laura Kearns; edited by Eddie Fournier

No part of this publication may be reproduced or distributed in any form or by any means, or stored in a database or retrieval system, except as permitted under Sections 107 or 108 of the U.S. Copyright Act, without prior written permission of the publisher. This book is printed on acid free paper.

Material in this book is for educational purposes only. This book is sold with the understanding that neither any of the authors or the publisher is engaged in rendering legal, accounting, investment, or any other professional service. Neither the publisher nor the authors assume any liability for any errors or omissions or for how this book or its contents are used or interpreted or for any consequences resulting directly or indirectly from the use of this book. For legal advice or any other, please consult your personal lawyer or the appropriate professional.

The views expressed by the individuals in this book (or the individuals on the cover) do not necessarily reflect the views shared by the companies they are employed by (or the companies mentioned in this book). The employment status and affiliations of authors with the companies referenced are subject to change.

Aspatore books may be purchased for educational, business, or sales promotional use. For information, please email AspatoreStore@thomson.com.

ISBN 1-59622-557-2   Library of Congress Control Number: 2006930701

For corrections, updates, comments or any other inquiries please email Aspatore.Editorial@thomson.com.

First Printing, 2006
10 9 8 7 6 5 4 3 2 1

Aspatore Books is the largest and most exclusive publisher of C-level executives (CEO, CFO, CTO, CMO, partner) from the world's most respected companies and law firms. Aspatore annually publishes a select group of C-level executives from the Global 1,000, top 250 law firms (partners and chairs), and other leading companies of all sizes. C-level Business Intelligence™, as conceptualized and developed by Aspatore Books, provides professionals of all levels with proven business intelligence from industry insiders—direct and unfiltered insight from those who know it best—as opposed to third-party accounts offered by unknown authors and analysts. Aspatore Books is committed to publishing an innovative line of business and legal books, those which lay forth principles and offer insights that, when employed, can have a direct financial impact on the reader's business objectives, whatever they may be. In essence, Aspatore publishes critical tools—need-to-read as opposed to nice-to-read books—for all business professionals.

To Bob Kelley, who contributed to this book with ideas and encouragement.

And to my wife, Kathleen, who has put up with this "type A" entrepreneur for over forty years.

All author royalties from the sale of this book are being donated to charity.

Contents

Introduction 9

Chapter 1: Establishing Your Vision: Focusing Your Resources to Reach a Goal 21

Chapter 2: Money: The Root of All Growth 37

Chapter 3: It's About Time 51

Chapter 4: Management of Relationships 79

Chapter 5: Process Management 89

Chapter 6: Defining the Context in Which We Work 101

Chapter 7: Interrelationships: Optimal Management of Competing Demands 121

Chapter 8: Checklist: Reviewing Your Leadership Strategies and Management Insights 135

About the Author 147

Introduction

The phrase "extending the runway" will be recognized by almost every venture capitalist and funded-company, C-level officer on Earth. Where the phrase came from is anyone's guess. I've been flying for over forty years, and we pilots know you can't extend a runway without plans, permits, perhaps some condemnation of land, relocation of perimeter roads, and who knows what else.

So, what about this title?

Well, if you're a pilot, you'll identify with the alternative titles we could have used, such as *Decreasing Accelerate-Stop Distance* or *Managing Fuel for Adequate Balanced Field Length*. Somehow, these didn't work. So we'll live with the common phrase, agreeing right at the start of this book that "extending the runway" is meant to indicate lengthening the time a company has to accelerate through break-even before running out of the green stuff.

We could easily have named this book *Running out of Runway*, with its negative connotation of the finality of the flight. And there certainly are stories in the aviation world to back up the notion, with air carrier craft piloted by well-trained crews failing in one way or another to terminate a flight before termination of the tarmac.

But this is a book about best practices for extending the usefulness of all available resources for companies that have received venture or angel funding, and rightfully should be attempting to stretch the funded dollars to create a valuable, profitable enterprise.

Over the years, I've found that management of every company, from startup to growth business, can make better use of five types of resources available to them. And, believe it or not, very few do so.

Let's get the entire thesis of this book out of the way on the first pages for those of you with limited attention spans. Here it is: You have at your fingertips five valuable commodities you can use to stretch your time to break-even and beyond. If you are about to close the cover and bail out of this book, at least note these five classes of resources: *time*, *money*, *process*, *context*, and *relationships*.

> **The five classes of critical resources: *time*, *money*, *process*, *context*, and *relationships*.**

You're now free to go—or read on. Warning: You are about to read lots about yourself that I am sure you will recognize. And you may not be entirely comfortable with yourself at times for having induced a crisis in your past or failing to cure one. I promise to make up for any of this discomfort with some great aviation stories, each to make a point and act as a proxy for you as crew member or pilot in command.

For you venture capitalists, many with your own jet or prop aircraft, you'll find lots of common threads and a new way of thinking about fragile young companies. And one of you out there surely is responsible for the unattributed phrase "extending the runway" and should be ashamed of yourself for misnaming the analogy and causing the rest of us to stop and explain your folly.

Now, let's get back to business. I've managed businesses or coached CEOs in this general class of small, funded companies for over fifty years, learning lots and witnessing many stories of success and woe during that time. It's time for me to share these stories all for the purpose of helping you process and gain insight into leveraging the various types of resources available to you—but often discounted or overlooked in the rush to build brand and business.

This book is not about learning the ins and outs of business management. It is about recognizing and leveraging your core resources so you never approach any of the five "resource bankruptcies" we'll explore in this book. It is about focusing your core competencies, pulling the right levers to avoid the pitfalls common to most businesses, while avoiding the drain on your critical resources including time and money.

I hope you will indulge me as I use my passion for aviation to illustrate the most critical points within this book. After over forty years as an active pilot, I admit to being as impassioned about flying as a business tool and passionate hobby as ever. Learning to fly back in the mid-1960s while running a growing entrepreneurial business, I was struck with the number of skills I could transfer from my aviation training to my business. This held true increasingly as I added ratings and classes to my license and was managing a more complex, expanding enterprise. There was a parallel in flying ever more complex, larger craft and managing the larger, more layered company.

Planning, tracking, thinking ahead while processing an overwhelming amount of data, considering the consequences of each action, starting a mission only after completing the planning process, and being reasonably confident of the outcome and alternatives are but several of the skills a pilot learns that apply equally in a business environment.

And then there is resource management. In aviation, we call it "crew resource management," a phrase used to describe the process of tapping into the sheer power of available resources inside the cockpit and on the ground—all aimed at helping the aircraft commander complete the mission safely. Growing to understand the concept that "business resource management" parallels its aviation counterpart closely, I've drawn upon numerous examples of good and bad resource management in the air to illustrate points within this book. So if nothing else, you should exit from this experience with some great aviation stories and a few factoids for use at cocktail parties. I've also called from memory a few stories of companies run by people I've coached who are perhaps a lot like you.

Over these years of flying, the planes have become more complex and the operating environment much less flexible, with new restrictions placed upon where and when a pilot can legally fly. Equate that with the mountain of recent business regulation, including the effects of Sarbanes-Oxley just for a start. September 11th and each aviation disaster seems to have given the government a new chance to add a restricted flying area or set of restrictive rules in the name of accident prevention and safety, kind of a Sarbanes-Oxley reaction to events and resulting legislation for the aviation world. Of course, the government has done the same thing in the business world during the same period in reaction to far too many business scandals—by enacting new laws, organizing departments within agencies, and creating rules and regulations, all aimed toward protecting the consumer, the employee, the outside investor.

The net result of these restrictions upon aviation and upon the business world as we know it is the same: the slow creation of a more complex environment requiring more knowledge, awareness, and skills to navigate successfully.

As I graduated from private to commercial pilot, from visual to instrument flight ratings, from singles to twins, each step called for more careful planning, more current knowledge, and more awareness of situations as they rapidly change in flight. "Stay in front of the plane" each Flight Safety simulator instructor or friendly flight instructor would say. "Don't let the plane fly you." Hmm. Sounds like advice for running our businesses, too.

Would you be surprised to find that 80 percent of all flying accidents are pilot-induced? And that half of those are weather-related? It wouldn't be hard to find a parallel to this amazing statistic in our venture-backed business world, supposing a similar percentage of early business failures are induced by command or leadership error as opposed to any perceived or real outside influence. And further, in a perfect world where we could precisely measure such things, I would bet that half of all business failures could conceivably be traced to inappropriate reactions to changes caused by external forces—just as half of all aviation accidents are weather-related, considering weather is classified as an external force. Well, that is until the pilot in command decides to take a chance on the weather rather than leaving the plane on the ground and pretty much guaranteeing to live for another day. Most of us like guarantees.

But some of us running businesses and some pilots just have to make the journey that day, risks be damned. In aviation, we call this "get there-it is," and it is a dangerous illness. Some pilots never shake this one, like a constant cold. Some inexperienced business leaders suffer from the same disease, not knowing when to push toward the goal and when to call a timeout to strengthen the troops for the charge.

In a perfect world, no entrepreneur—no professional manager—would take control of a business and barrel down the runway without so much as a plan or a briefing.

But the world is not perfect. Planes do crash. Businesses surely fail. Lives are altered. And the prepared, trained, and skilled carry on after an ever-so-brief look back to learn from the bad luck and poor judgment from their past performances and those of their contemporaries.

So in this book you're going to get a dose of something pilots have been doing for years. Pilots as a class fanatically read about the published stories of fatal mistakes made by their more unlucky brethren. Aviation magazines carry monthly summaries and analyses of aircraft accidents and incidents, all in the name of learning from the mistakes of others. Most pilots read these columns religiously, looking for similarities to their personal environment: the same type of aircraft, same pilot experience level, and same area of the country. Few ever dare say, "That couldn't happen to me."

One of the longer-running monthly columns in *Flying Magazine* is entitled "I Learned About Flying from That." And even more to the point, *Flying Magazine* prints another monthly column entitled "Aftermath," and *Business and Commercial Aviation* publishes "Cause and Circumstance." Each magazine reprints actual cockpit and controller conversation through to the moment of the crash (as published from cockpit recorder tapes released by the Federal Aviation Administration) and then attempts to analyze the causes of aviation calamities from the words and actions of the pilots whose final moments revealed clues to the cause.

You'll quickly note that most of the examples and business cases I cite are from the technology arena. I've done so purposely, since that's the arena where most venture capitalists and I play—our sandbox. It's also an arena with problems that tend to be more complex than many types of business, made more so by the rapid pace of obsolescence and downward pricing pressures endemic to technology-based businesses. Time is compressed in every facet of a technology-centric business where product life cycles are horribly short, margins sometimes paper thin, and competition from anywhere in the world able to overwhelm a business quickly. But the lessons learned from the technology sector are applicable most anywhere in the business world. And since business cycles are shorter, fixes and patches to a business tend to show results (positive or negative) sooner than in many industries.

Most every venture capitalist will agree that near-fatal mistakes are magnified in the technology environment. Even the most visible and famous managers of the business world have later been found guilty by the "court of common hindsight" of missing the dominant trend through misjudgment and inability to see the changes in product-customer context. I know you'll recognize most of the following famous gaffs and misjudgments by earlier peers of ours, but it is humbling to review the best of them one more time...

In 1943, you'll recall that Thomas Watson Sr., chairman of IBM, stated: *"I think there is a world market for maybe five computers."*

In 1957, Prentice Hall's editor in charge of business books was quoted as saying: *"I have traveled the length and breadth of this country and talked with the best people, and I can assure you that data processing is a fad that won't last out the year."*

> **Even the most visible and famous managers in the business world have later been found guilty by the "court of common hindsight" of missing the dominant trend through misjudgment and inability to see the changes in product-customer context.**

Ken Olson, founder of Digital Equipment Corporation and one of the very first to produce a mini-computer that would later open the power of mainframe computing to small and middle-size businesses, never lived down his 1977 oft-quoted statement that: *"There is no reason anyone would want a computer in their home."*

Even Bill Gates, one of the most visible leaders of the personal computer revolution, fell off the technology turnip truck and into the obsolescence trap with his 1981 statement: *"640K ought to be enough for anybody."* Perhaps that was true in the context of DOS and the times; it was just famously not visionary.

Remember, too, that Intel started life as a memory company, switching to processors to avert the disaster that surely would have been theirs to live out as memory prices slid off the charts through the 1980s.

Of course, the high-tech world is not the only one where leaders have missed great opportunities knocking at their door. You've heard about Fred Smith's Yale University professor who reacted to Smith's master's thesis laying out what would soon become Federal Express: *"The concept is interesting and well formed, but in order to earn better than a 'C,' the idea must be feasible."*

"Who the hell wants to hear actors talk?" asked Harry Warner of Warner Brothers in 1927. And a representative from Decca Records is purported to have stated about the Beatles: *"We don't like their sound, and guitar music is on the way out."*

My favorite quote as we tour this museum of gaffs comes from Charles H. Duell, U.S. commissioner of patents, who, prognosticating in 1899, must hold the record for business foresight. Your recall the now infamous: *"Everything that can be invented has been invented."*

Maybe we can forgive these guys for missing their mark. In 1927, business was so brisk at movie houses that Mr. Warner would be thinking of how not to obsolete his golden goose, silent pictures. Well, true, unless he could have had the foresight to see that someone else could take away his business within just three years—if he failed to adapt to "talkies." And Bill Gates was probably recalling that he wrote his Basic language for the Altair 8800 using just 4K of memory just four years earlier when he made the statement that "640K ought to be enough."

Ken Olsen had helped to create a revolution in computing during the seven years prior to his remark, and he too might have been a victim of wishful thinking, hoping the mini-computer would be able to feed his fortunes forever. Many of us do recall asking, "How could we use a personal computer at home? Saving cooking recipes?" We couldn't imagine that storing recipes and keeping the family checkbook could ever justify owning a personal computer. That makes us guilty of lack of vision, or better yet, perfect candidates for a visionary to come and lead us to need, not want, computers for every member of our family over time.

So predictably, soon after Olsen's pronouncement, the first "killer application" was born, changing the perception of the technology world forever. With a killer application like SuperCalc (remember the original spreadsheet for eight-bit computers?), we found all kinds of liberating business and home uses for the computer by creating our own content or data that could be forever sorted and tumbled and treated to "What if?" scenarios. And with word processing and later Scott Cook's "Quicken" personal financial system, the killer application found its way into the home and office. Millions of us discovered that we just couldn't do without spreadsheets, word processing, financial management, and Internet access. And, thanks to Fred Smith, millions of us soon discovered that we could not do without overnight package delivery.

So part of this book is devoted to finding and then taking advantage of the "prevailing winds" of change that provide business-killing challenges and industry-creating opportunities, sometimes simultaneously. We'll explore the thesis that failure to see the dominant force that will soon change a business is to fail to see the movement of the *context* in which we operate. And failure to follow within the context envelope is a sure setup for failure of the business itself in time.

Other forms of mistakes—from simple money mismanagement, to failure to foresee the results of a series of actions, to trying to "do it all alone"—ultimately prove fatal. Just look at the number of business bankruptcies filed each year. Increasing at a rate of over 30 percent per year adjusted for business cycles, businesses fail at alarming rates.

> **Failure to see the dominant force that will soon change a business is to fail to see the movement of the *context* in which we operate. And failure to follow within the context envelope is a sure setup for failure of the business itself in time.**

We almost called this book *Avoiding Fatal Mistakes*. But our journey is beyond just the avoidance of mistakes; it is to discover and embrace the opportunities we may or may not recognize as they occur. It's about knowing how to apportion resources, including that valuable commodity time, while stretching the funds invested in, generated from, or remaining within the enterprise. It's about knowing and capitalizing upon the power of relationships in getting the big breaks as well as getting things done. It's about being very certain we know the process before attempting the adventure. (Is it time to jog your memory: *money, time, context, process, and relationships*? Just checking.)

And, perhaps most important, it's about knowing and believing in the goal. In aviation, the goal is simple: *complete the flight*. Of course there are other, less urgent goals: safety, comfort, and flight efficiency. But in business, the goals enumerated by management are often more obscure—or missing altogether. So we'll explore the need for and measurement of goals as we examine the strategies needed to extend your runway.

There are some simple methods of strategic planning in the use of management's resources available to us in order to get the most benefit from what are always constrained resources in any size of business, and to avoid fatal mistakes by better defining the possible outcomes for the actions we take.

Far less than 1 percent of all growing companies will ever go public. And history is not often kind to small businesses with big ambitions. Many have and will be caught in the web of financial bankruptcy or be significantly sidetracked by other kinds of *resource bankruptcy* along the way.

Resource bankruptcy?

Here's a new phrase for an old set of problems. Running out of resources (including money) is a serious threat to be managed as carefully as managing growth. It is a business equivalent of a pilot hearing the engine sputter when you're flying 1,000 feet over one of the Great Lakes. The pilot worries over whether the problem is real or imagined, given the inhospitable environment below. Pilots refer to this phenomenon as "automatic rough" where, whenever we worry, the engine seems to run as if it is about to fall apart. Thoughts go to whether we can fix a real or imagined problem while still in the air. Is there someone at the other end of a radio call who can give some quick and effective advice? Or is it time to think of staying upright in the survival raft?

Resource bankruptcy, which can and does include financial bankruptcy, is the recognition that you've just become unable to continue "flying your craft." You've run out of runway ahead or altitude below, and it's time to plan to terminate your flight a little prematurely. This unhappy circumstance may face you either because of pilot error or equipment failure. But the effect will be the same. (Yes, I know: *"Any landing you can walk away from is a good landing."*)

However, this book is about staying in the air—keeping the business going and growing. So let's use this book to learn to recognize the symptoms of resource bankruptcy and to find insights to avoid or recover from these worst of all possible plagues upon early-stage businesses.

Bankruptcy of any kind infers that you lose some or all control of your business. Often, it delivers the added blow of evaporating all of your equity value, rendering the past investment of time and money valueless, except for the expensive experience you've gained.

All forms of resource bankruptcy usually happen so slowly that those in control don't fully realize they're losing that control and running out of options—until there are no good options left.

Companies seldom suddenly go out of business. Few regulatory, competitive, or management-driven events could make a company bankrupt overnight. Barring acts of God, it usually takes more than one bad decision or bad break to bring down a business. We learn that in flying, too. Almost always, by identifying and fixing the problems early, flying is a forgiving art. But let small problems combine with other small problems to become one big problem, and your lack of vigilance can easily bring down your plane.

One great truism is that experience is a powerful but inefficient teacher, tending to give the test first and teach the lessons later. Unfortunately, business managers usually find this out later rather than sooner, and at considerable expense.

> **All forms of resource bankruptcy usually happen so slowly that those in control don't fully realize they're losing that control and running out of options—until there are no good options left.**

Few of us have enough time or money to make a lot of mistakes and still stay in the game. And investors are increasingly volatile in dealing with those who do. Voting with their money or their board seats, venture investors today don't wait too long to replace the deadwood to protect their stake, even if the timbers shed are the limbs of the founders.

There's a story about the young man who climbed the mountain to ask the Oracle:

> *"How do I get to be a good pilot?"*
> "Good decisions," the Oracle said.
> *"How do I learn to make good decisions?"* the young pilot asked.
> "Experience," said the wise old man.
> *"Well, how do I get experience?"* the pilot pressed.
> "From making bad decisions," answered the sage.

Good judgment comes from experience, which comes from bad judgment—a quote attributable to Barry LePatner.

That is true of most learning in our society, but there is little tolerance for this kind of learning in experience-critical situations. We'll address these critical situations from the worst case scenarios, which we'll call "experience-related bankruptcies." And you can use these to calibrate your situation. Then *you* can determine whether you're dealing with just the afternoon breeze or the dark insides of a thunderstorm.

If you've ever managed a business enterprise that performed marginally or even poorly, and if you find you are all too familiar with one or more of the five forms of resource bankruptcy you'll uncover in this book, you might smile with the special insight that you've seen this one before. And if you're new to the management game, here are some of the tips and traps that should make your work more effective over time.

Strap on your parachute if you're insecure. Just jump in the plane if you're bold. Do a careful walk-around inspection if you're trained and cautious.

It's time to go flying…

1

Establishing Your Vision: Focusing Your Resources to Reach a Goal

"That what is true of business and politics is gloriously true of professions, the arts and crafts, the sciences, the sports. That the best picture has not been painted; the greatest poem is still unsung; the mightiest novel remains to be written; the divinest music has not been conceived even by Bach. In science, probably 99 percent of the knowable has (yet) to be discovered." – Lincoln Steffens, October 1932

Each new aircraft designed today begins life at a drawing board or CAD station designed for a specific task where it will excel at its job. Design of an aircraft is always a tradeoff between weight, speed, and load carrying capacity, just as businesses are started with a specific niche market or solution in mind or, if properly launched, with a vision for the enterprise.

Vision is everything. Businesses formed and run without it meander their way through the years, usually as examples of enterprises lost in mediocrity. Those entrepreneurs and managers who have taken the time to shape a true, compelling vision for their enterprise have many times changed the world. Bill Gates's "a computer for every desk" vision is one of this generation's greatest examples of a simple, easy-to-grasp, compelling vision for a company and even for an industry.

> ***Vision is everything.*** **Businesses formed and run without it meander their way through the years, usually as examples of enterprises lost in mediocrity.**

In this chapter, we'll test your vision for your enterprise by probing it for context and capability of your enterprise to execute. Then we'll provide some tools for you to use or modify as you explore your vision.

But first, how about a great aviation story that illustrates how an entrepreneur's vision can become the centerpiece for amazing accomplishments? Here's one of my favorites…

In December of 1986, Dick Rutan and Jeana Yeager took off on an around-the-world odyssey in the Burt Rutan-designed Voyager, an extremely lightweight composite plastic aircraft designed for one function: to be the first aircraft ever to fly around the world without refueling. Nine days later, the two pilots landed back at their takeoff point with but several hours of fuel left in the tanks. The plane now rests in the Smithsonian Museum, hanging from the ceiling, a tribute to the vision, focus, and courage of its creators and pilots.

That aircraft was created with a singular purpose. All of the elements of design and all of the planning for the flight revolved around that singular purpose. Once the job was completed, there was no frontier left for that particular craft to explore, and a graceful retirement was appropriate. On the other hand, Burt Rutan went on to design more aircraft that would advance aviation technology, based in part upon the things he learned from Voyager, including a subsequent single-pilot craft for the same function, in which Steve Fawcett flew his record-breaking non-stop flight around the world in 2005.

Considering the state of the aviation industry at the time and taking into account his core competencies, Rutan defined a vision that congealed a small crew of dedicated fanatics for two years, making the most efficient use then possible of the group's limited resources—time and money.

In this section, we are going to share tools to explore whether your business opportunity is mediocre, average, or superior, and whether your assessment of your business is likely to be the same as that of your investors. We'll define some of the things about your company that will attract interest or conversely repel investors and other stakeholders as they examine your opportunity.

Establishing Your Vision

It should be understood that, as technology advances, business opportunities that were attractive when conceived may become dead-end opportunities at some point simply because of technological obsolescence. Therefore, one of the first priorities of an outside analyst—whether investor, potential advisor, or candidate executive—is to assess the position of the company in relation to the life span of its key technologies.

It is also important to gauge your business and its opportunities in light of the trends in your industry, in society, and in technology. And that's not easy, especially if you are caught up in the moment, creating a product or enterprise to take advantage of an opportunity opened by competitive misjudgment, excess customer demand in your niche, or product/service fad of the moment.

I have my own story to illustrate this one, and it addresses the context of a rapidly changing industry where new product development was not given enough credence by existing enterprises. Remember Jack Warner purposely turning his back on the talking motion picture, wanting with all his being to extend his investment in equipment and content in production and in the can, all silent pictures?

I was a teenage entrepreneur, starting my first real business at the age of sixteen, producing phonograph records of school and college musical performances to sell to families of the performers—sort of a vanity press for the audio business. I operated the business from my bedroom. Working and growing the record business through college, then making a full-time enterprise of it upon graduation, the business built its own state-of-the-art phonograph manufacturing plant and flourished. After adding a division that produced "oldie but goodie" albums of all-time-great hits for sale through radio and television advertising and another division to produce popular records for sale to the public, the growing company went public in 1971.

In late 1974, I sold my interest in the then-public company so I could move on into the then-hot new mini-computer software business. The move wasn't made because I had any negative insight into the future of the phonograph record manufacturing business, but because I sensed that the software business was about to become the right place to be for the next generation.

And I was right...and very lucky to have vacated the record manufacturing business when I did.

In the year I sold my interest in the record company, tape cassettes were just beginning to siphon sales at the retail level from plastic phonograph record albums. Within five years, the long-playing phonograph record album was all but dead—a victim of better technology in the form of the cassette. The thirty record pressing plants that existed in Hollywood and its environs during the 1960s declined to just one remaining plant.

The phonograph record manufacturing industry had recreated the old "buggy whip manufacturing" story eighty years later. Back then, the new technology appeared in the form of the horseless carriage—the automobile.

Those who invested in plants and equipment late in the life cycle of either industry were burned beyond recognition in the crash that soon followed, because they failed to capture the perspective of technology trends. No new innovations—no marketing brilliance—could reverse either technology trend.

Companies have life cycles of their own, usually but not always influenced by the cycles of the industry they serve. Even in a nearly dead industry, a small player with a niche market can grow handsomely for a while. And many an early entrant hangs on to a dying business for emotional reasons unwilling to see a vision die. Or for personal security: "What will I do with my life now?"

Companies are more likely to thrive in a growing market than in a declining one. Company life cycles should be viewed in light of industry trends. And investments of time and money should be made with—not counter to—the prevailing winds of technology. Or, as Damon Runyon, a colorful mid-century writer wrote: *"The race may not always be to the swift, nor the victory to the strong; but that is how you bet."* (He's also the one who said *"Trust, but verify."*)

How would your business opportunity be measured by a professional investor, a venture capitalist, or the public marketplace? There are guidelines such people often use to compare a business under evaluation against their criteria for investment. Although these will change between individuals and companies, here is a reasonable attempt to generalize them...

> **Companies are more likely to thrive in a growing market than in a declining one. Company life cycles should be viewed in light of industry trends. And investments of time and money should be made with—not counter to—the prevailing winds of technology.**

1. Where is your business in terms of your market opportunity life cycle?

Are you still producing the same product you or your competitors produced five years ago, failing to take advantage of new technologies? Are your competitors starting to gain market share with innovative products or enhancements to existing products? Or is your product at the leading edge of a hot market just revealing itself?

2. How large is the total market for your product?

If the total market as you have defined it is under $200 million of strong annual demand worldwide, then the burden of proof falls upon you to prove your ability to truly dominate that market through some combinations of core competencies and high barriers to entry.

3. Is your business capable of becoming a dominant player in the marketplace?

A small player with the potential to capture less than 30 percent of any emerging marketplace will be buffeted by the price, advertising, positioning, and expansionary wars fought by larger players with greater resources. There is nothing wrong with having a small part of a large market if you are able to grow and finance the operation without investment from venture capitalists seeking comfort as well as potential. In other words, entrepreneurial businesses are good when the entrepreneur can make a niche for himself or herself and money from the operation. However, that could be a "lifestyle" opportunity, one not suitable for outside investors looking for a much higher upside. A superior business opportunity generally requires more resources and a larger potential market share of at least 50 percent, even if you define the market as a smaller niche that can be dominated by your company.

4. Have you created high barriers to entry to prevent competition?

Do you have a patentable product or subsystem? Do you have the certification or recommendation of a major trade group to the exclusion of competitors? Is the development cycle so long that there is a broad window of time before others could copy your idea? Do you have a development team that can quickly swamp new competitors by continuously moving faster than their counterparts to provide consumer-defined "better" products?

5. Are the margins strong enough to encourage continued research by the company to maintain leadership?

For a company with measurable research costs, gross profit on product sales should exceed 50 percent of gross revenues (70 percent in some cases), while operating profit before interest and taxes should exceed 10 to 20 percent if the business has been selling product for longer than a year or two (unless the achievement of dominant market share is the principal short-term goal of the enterprise). Another measure of corporate health is gross profit per employee, which should exceed $150,000 in a growing company with a superior opportunity. This number is heavily influenced by two things: whether production labor is treated as fixed or variable cost and whether the company is in the early stage of product sale and therefore able to extract higher prices for new products not yet commoditized. Some small startups use their limited resources for both development and production in the early stages, often not recognizing the true (higher) cost of production.

Some more sophisticated venture-backed businesses test the "personal productivity ratio" of their employees by assessing the gross profit by

Establishing Your Vision

department, comparing it against the labor costs for each department. This requires an elaborate apportioning of revenues between sales, marketing, research, and other departments, which may not be worth the effort needed. A personal productivity ratio of .40 is considered excellent, indicating that payroll costs do not exceed 40 percent of gross profit. One purpose for this measure is to see whether the research is in proportion to the company's ability to sustain that research without continuous outside investment.

For distribution companies, the gross margins run much lower, often as low as 15 percent. Although revenue per employee in such segments may rise as high as $1 million per employee and over, the fair test is again to test gross profit per employee, which should still exceed $150,000, as difficult as that may seem to some with razor-thin margins.

> **The core competency of a company resides in its knowledge of its marketplace and the ability to translate that knowledge into products that fit the market and are well received by customer prospects.**

6. *Can the business grow to at least $50 million in revenues within five years?*

Venture capitalists see many new business plans each week. Some are well crafted but dull. A few—very few—exude a vision for the enterprise that is compelling and believable. But many of these cannot make a case for a business that can grow to $50 million in five years, if ever. Those that cannot find a way to believably create businesses of this size are not interesting to the vast majority of venture capitalists. That's just a fact.

7. *Do you have a world-class management team?*

Most venture capital investments are made as a result of relationships, not business plans. Good management (hopefully with a proven track record of growing great companies) always carries more weight in the investment decision process than any other controllable factor. If your management team is weak, or young, or thin, you should look to beef up this area early in your preparations for growth and before seeking outside financing (unless you are willing to give up 60 or more percent of your company to a "seed-round" venture capitalist).

8. Do you have a world-class research and development team?

The core competency of a company resides in its knowledge of its marketplace and the ability to translate that knowledge into products that fit the market and are well received by customer prospects. The development team leads that effort and acts as a repository for that core of knowledge within the company.

9. Can you translate an idea into a product quickly and establish market leadership?

A great idea fails the test if it cannot quickly be made into a great product or service in a growing market. And a great product or service that is one among many is of little interest to outside investors.

> **Many a good idea has been hatched and funded without a clue as to how to find customers in sufficient number to make the idea a success.**

10. Is your market identifiable and accessible?

Do you know where your customers are and how to reach them? Many a good idea has been hatched and funded without a clue as to how to find customers in sufficient number to make the idea a success. For business plans I see with this obvious core vision missing or fuzzy, I've dubbed this the "*Field of Dreams* factor." ("Build it, and they will come.") The truly great market is one in which your customers express an "urgent demand" for your product or are quick to purchase once you have led them to understand it.

11. Can the company support the product once in the market?

If the support cost is so high in time and cost that the product could never become profitable, the idea dies until a solution can be found. The problem is that, often, no one knows what the support requirements will be until it is too late and an overly complex or bug-ridden product is released. There are few second chances for a product that is released with problems—without overwhelming financial and public relations cost.

> **There are few second chances for a product released with problems—without overwhelming financial and public relations cost.**

12. Does the company have a believable business plan?

This is two questions in one. Many companies seek help or launch operations without a plan at all. Others draw a plan no one can believe. Both usually fail.

13. Is the idea—is the company—able to generate a reasonable profit?

Long term, the idea of investing in a company with no profit potential makes little sense. Yes, biotech investments are made by knowledgeable investors who expect no profit for up to ten years. Some investments in interactive multimedia and Internet-based businesses are being made with the same expectation. Those, such as the successful initial public offering for Netscape Communications in 1995, are absolutely exceptions to the rule. Make money; make friends.

14. Is there an exit strategy for the investor over time?

Venture capitalists are not banks. They begin their involvement with a company with the tacit or open question: "How will we get our money (and profit) out someday?" There are many forms of planned exits for professional investors:

- Private offerings of stock
- Initial public offerings
- Company buy-back of investors' shares
- Planned sale of the company
- Planned merger with publicly traded company

- Co-investor buy/sell agreement
- Management leveraged buyout plan
- Employee stock option plan planned buyout

These exit strategies and more are often discussed by investors and founder-entrepreneurs even before an initial commitment is made. The founder who expects cash from anyone other than a family member or friend with blind faith will face this reality.

The window of time most knowledgeable investors look for is three to seven years from investment to liquidity. Venture capital money is often said to be costly, not because it carries a high service cost in interest and fees, although it may, but because venture fund investors target at least a 35 percent per year increase in their investments over the period or a ten times return at a liquidity event. This aggressive number is not surprising, considering the risk they take and the number of investments they make that end up losing value.

Many entrepreneurs today start their businesses looking for security, individual self-determination, flexible work schedules, or a myriad of other very personal reasons. To these people, this short discussion will have been irrelevant for the short term. But sometime, even the lone entrepreneur will need to consider an exit strategy to fit into an estate plan.

How do you go about crafting a vision of your own? There are many good tools to help you and your co-managers find your way from fuzzy goals to sharp vision. One of those I use often in business planning is the question chain. You get together with your best advisors and co-managers, dedicate at least half a day to start, and ask, "What if…?" and "What then…?"

Over the years, I've developed a set of questions to lead management through the exercise of finding and formalizing the vision. At the companies where I've used this tool, often acting as facilitator of a several-day retreat designed to immerse management into the process, the tool has been referred to as "The 100 Questions"—even if the actual number falls somewhat short. A sample format for such a meeting follows. You can skip to the end of the chapter if you wish. Hopefully, you'll return to copy this and shape it to fit your needs by developing your own questions more

Establishing Your Vision

appropriate to your enterprise when you embark upon your own vision-defining or -refining planning process…

The "100" Questions for Use in Your Planning Session

1. The Global Market Niche We Address
Where is the opportunity?
Who has already exploited this and with what resources?
Is there a place for us to create a place for ourselves?
Can we excel with lower cost, higher quality, or innovation?
What are the risks of execution in this niche?
Do we have the resources to attempt to compete?
What technology or competitor could come along and surprise us?
Have we sufficient intellectual property protection to withstand attacks if we are successful?

2. The Business of the Company
Can we describe our business vision to a third party in one minute or less?
What makes us different from our actual and potential competitors?
What is the size of the potential marketplace, domestic and international?
Are we using all available channels of distribution to enhance our reach globally?
How does the marketplace perceive our strengths?
How do we perceive our strengths?
How does the market perceive our weaknesses?
What do we know to be our weaknesses?
How can we capitalize upon these strengths?
Is our product niche too narrow to make a big opportunity of this business?
What prevents others from duplicating our strengths? (i.e., What are the barriers to entry into our niche?)

3. The Marketplace
How large is our defined marketplace in potential annual revenue (to all companies)?
Who is the perceived competition?

What is the estimated industry sales volume in our niche? (i.e., How much of the available market is serviced today?)
How can we be perceived as a leader within this niche?
What does the competition do better than we do?
What do we do better than the competition?
Is our pricing strategy appropriate? How do we know?
What measures of success do we expect from our sales force?
How can we increase the revenues per salesperson through any action or resource we do not now use?
What area of our potential market have we ignored?
How do we exploit the competition's weaknesses?
Are we using all effective vehicles for advertising?
Have we made it easy for our customers to find us and buy from us?
What is our revenue goal for each of the next three years?
How do we achieve that goal?
What is the cost of achieving that goal?
Do we have the resources to make that effort?

4. The Product

Are we as efficient as we could be in producing our product or service?
Do we use technology to reduce cost and better communicate with our suppliers?
What is our potential gross profit? What is our present actual gross profit? Per employee?
How much more money and time would it take to achieve our potential gross profit?
Is our technology "state of the art"?
What resources would we need to make us above the rest?
Is our product advantage perceived as based upon technology, price, or quality?
What more can we do to differentiate us from all the rest chasing us or leading us?

5. The Company Structure

Are we structured correctly today to grow this business?
Have we identified any bottlenecks in the operation, in people, or in resources, that we can remove to increase productivity?
Where are our other organizational weaknesses?

Establishing Your Vision

What changes would we need to make to achieve the growth projected?
What has limited our growth in the past?
Is acquisition a logical growth strategy?

6. Our People

Is our pay structure competitive? How do we know?
Do we attract bright, A-rated talent?
Is our recruiting appropriate to reach the best and brightest candidates?
Are there sources for recruiting that we've ignored?
How can we best create or enhance appropriate incentives for our salespeople that match our corporate goals?
What incentives do we offer for others in our organization? Do they align with our corporate goals?
Do we use the best available method of communication with the field force and capture of their activities for management and accounting use?
How could we improve upon our internal communication? Tools? Process?

7. Marketing

Do we have the proper marketing talent?
How do we present our collateral to the market? Is it appropriate and cost-effective?
Is our corporate and product marketing focus "fuzzy" or "precise"?

8. Other Issues of Concern

9. What Is Our Enterprise Vision?

10. Do We Have a Concise Mission Statement? An Elevator Pitch?

11. What Is Our Most Important Three-Year Goal?

12. What Are at Least Five Strategies and Five Tactics for Each to Achieve Our Three-Year Goal?

13. Can We Break These into Functional Areas So Each Department has Goals Aligned with Our Corporate Goal?

This format is certainly not unique or unbending. The exercise itself is more important than the form it takes. Note that most of the questions in the format above require only a single answer.

About Mission, Goals, and Strategies

There has been lots of talk these past years about audacious goals that galvanize a company into performance way beyond expectation. Certainly, venture capitalist investors like to probe such opportunities for a realistic chance of success over time. And we'll assume you are reading this book because you have already passed through the initial test of creating your basic vision, selling others on it, and starting down the path of execution.

Bill Conlin, retired president of CalComp Inc., a Lockheed company, often told the story that he used to drive in to work each Monday morning as if he were arriving at a new job for the first time. He would ask himself, "What would I do with this business if I were new to the job, had no preconceived notions, and could execute a brilliant plan with this team?" It takes a bold manager to continually think ahead about reinventing the business to meet the ever-changing world market. Andy Grove did a superior job of describing his past experiences with Intel in his book, *Only the Paranoid Survive*. Not one of us is good enough to rest on a decaying vision in an ever-changing environment and succeed in the long run.

Scott McNealy, founding CEO of Sun Microsystems, surely remained in his post for a much too-long sixteen years, in the end unable to bring himself to reduce his workforce to match Sun's diminishing market presence after the Internet boom. It took a change at the helm in 2006, when Jonathon Schwartz stepped into the position and immediately moved to reduce Sun's 37,500-person workforce by up to 5,000 people, to restore profitability.

What would you change if you were a new CEO coming into your enterprise for the first time, with no strings or ties to the past?

Conlin also took his mission statement and aimed it precisely. He recognized that mission statements are often just words worried over by teams for weeks or months that rarely are remembered by those using them. Worse yet, most mission statements are too long, too wordy, and too

Establishing Your Vision

homogenous. Those statements that are truly memorable and usable become icons in a sea of mediocrity. So what mission statement did Conlin and his team end up with? *"Customer first, always."* There are other great examples of outstanding mission statements, such as FedEx's *"Absolutely, positively overnight,"* that we remember as consumers, shaping our view of the company and its product to the exclusion of competitors.

> **What would you change if you were a new CEO coming into your enterprise for the first time, with no strings or ties to the past?**

How about strategies and tactics? Every company deserves and needs a roadmap for its management and its stakeholders. I've chosen the format known as "OST: objectives, strategies, and tactics" for this illustration. There are several other formats that are equally effective. But the format is not important. Much more important is the effort by senior management to break down strategic goals into goals for each department and each employee that align with these goals. Much more important is the development of tools and discipline to measure progress toward reaching these goals and using those tools regularly.

Trite statements do not mean they are not important or true statements. We achieve what we can measure. We expect what we inspect. We cannot achieve a goal that is unstated.

> **We cannot achieve a goal that is unstated.**

My favorite senior executives develop a sixth sense about their businesses. They sniff out metrics that are easy to measure and constant in availability, so they know when something begins to go awry with the business. Some have great one-page reports they use, often daily, to measure progress and problems. Some are lucky enough to have a dashboard that draws constant data from the corporate database, pointing out excursions beyond the norm for attention. All can tell you immediately which five or six measures of corporate health they use to watch over their complex enterprise, and how they ferret out the information to feed their habit. If you do not have command over such a concise flow of information to help you intuitively recognize when problems are bubbling under the surface, make an immediate note to focus upon this task at the next opportunity.

What if your vision requires resources you do not have and could not grab? How would you stretch those resources you do have to inch ever closer to achieving the goals you've set? When and how do you recognize when you are failing to make use of resources that could extend your runway or ensure your success?

It's time to explore the five classes of resources you've already memorized, and raise your awareness of the upsides and downsides associated with each.

Let's start with my favorite: money. Seems we all need more. And if we had enough, we'd never worry about the end of the runway. Money does mask lots of mistakes. But we do pay for those mistakes with dilution, risk, higher cost of funds in later rounds if less than successful, and career-breaking hits to our reputation if unsuccessful. So let's examine some of the traps of having too much and the risks of having too little of this resource in our next chapter.

2

Money: The Root of All Growth

"May you have the hindsight to know where you've been, the foresight to know where you're going, and the insight to know when you're going too far." – An old Irish toast

"There is nothing more frightful than ignorance in action." – Johann Wolfgang von Goethe

It's natural to be optimistic at the start of a new relationship. Angel and venture investors would not have written the check if they thought the company, management, and plan was unworthy of their investment. And most projections from entrepreneurs or management were discounted, but the premise was accepted nonetheless.

I've written many of those checks, joined many of those newly constituted boards, begun to dig into the layers below those so carefully uncovered during the due diligence process, and been shocked. Or perhaps slowly boiled, like Mark Twain's story of the frog in the kettle. If the true potential of a business, lack of resources, attacks from outside, and misadventures of management all come out slowly over time after the investment, it is easy to succumb to the frog-in-the-kettle life-threatening situation. Boiling as I smile.

Most venture capitalists will expect that their money invested will be used to spin up the activity in order to prove the viability of the plan, force the company to refine its original plan as circumstances change or reveal themselves, find the sweet spot niche, and make the explosive run for the gold. No venture capitalist will expect that their investment will be wasted through inefficient and wasteful habits of management. Yet I have seen more misuses of invested funds soon after the receipt of funds than I would want to see in a lifetime.

During the Internet bubble and as recently as the last Series B round in which I participated, management purchased Aeron chairs, expensive furniture, and a whole backlog of technology far beyond need or expectation. It seems a cliché: receive the cash and immediately unleash the floodgate of pent-up demand for new notebook computers, backup servers, enterprise software, and more. The business did not change between the moment before and the moment after the receipt of the big check. But the mindset of management somehow is almost always distorted by the bulging balance sheet to spend and spend.

Let me ask a telling question: Did the corporate circumstances change overnight because of the funding? And in answering, don't confuse the balance sheet change with a change in corporate opportunity.

There is quite a difference between reckless spending and planned investment in product development, marketing, or sales. I address the former—reckless misuse of funds early in the cycle when funds seem plentiful. Let's speak about the obvious. Money is power. With new funding and lots of runway, management feels the power that comes from having new options in the use of funds, new ability to reduce pressure from vendors who once were put off but now expect immediate payment, from employees including senior managers themselves, suddenly expecting to be paid no less than market rates and perks. The usual result is a sudden increase in overhead, often far more than scheduled, none of which contributes directly to growth of the enterprise.

So let's put some rules on the table up front.

Never Run Out of Money

Is this obvious? Not as obvious as you'd think. Circumstances often mask the drainage of cash in mysterious ways. A company on whose board I sat reacted to an attack by a salesperson from a competitor who told customers of our company that they should stop doing business with our company because the salesperson's company was suing our company "for all they're

Money: The Root of all Growth

worth" because of patent infringement. Customers stopped or at least paused to examine the claim, greatly reducing revenues for several painful months. Our board agreed with management that a lawsuit against the competitor was an appropriate response. Over $800,000 in legal fees later, a settlement was reached between the two companies, and our cash situation was in peril as a result. Slow boil, like the frog in the kettle.

So it is worth repeating in capitals: NEVER RUN OUT OF MONEY. Money represents power and preserves corporate value. The same corporation before and after running out of cash is a very different company with a very different enterprise value. There is no time to work through the proposition that new investment is an option, or sale of the company at distressed prices can be avoided if new cash (expensive cash) is not immediately available.

> **NEVER RUN OUT OF MONEY. Money represents power and preserves corporate value.**

Planned cash-out dates are always watched carefully, and a good company's board will begin actions to see that cash is not drained too quickly near the end of the runway. Obvious as that seems, I have seen far too many companies fail to account for involuntary expenses and lose control of cash at the most critical of times.

Let's speak about one basic philosophy of monetary planning that every company's board should discuss early on after an injection of new cash. I'll label it the "push/pull" discussion. Those of you who recall your college economics study of John Maynard Keynes and his theories of macro and micro economics will recall "demand pull or cost push" referring to the two most common drivers of inflation. Demand pull: Prices are bid upward as consumers bid up the price of scarce resources, increasing the cost of living merely because of the scarcity of those resources. Cost push: Labor costs, materials costs, energy costs, and an unfavorable exchange rate all serve to drive up prices, causing inflation to ripple throughout the system.

Let's take a short leap and apply the terms not to inflation but to the way in which you and your board approach planned spending of your capital. The terms take on an entirely new meaning. Cost push: We spend (and spend) our newfound corporate resources even before the market shows increased interest (demand) for our product. Demand pull: We spend to seed the effort to market through product development, wise marketing, and targeted sales force build-out, but nothing more. We maneuver in every way possible to be pulled by the market into spending more, but only as needed. We build out our call center and add to the research and development staff. We finally start looking for that new office—only as a result of customer demand.

Which is the safest alternative? Most of us will favor demand pull even as we warn of the dangers of being ill-equipped to respond to customer service needs early in the cycle of demand. The dangers of cost push are great. Sometimes demand never does show up in the system, no matter which levers we pull and how much we spend on research and development or marketing. I've seen it time and again. Many great products or services have been pushed into the market with a great marketing effort and good salespeople evangelizing a new product into a market that is just not responsive or ready for the offering. I'd much rather deal with the effects of early customer service pressure than spend my way through the company's cash pushing a product or service uphill further and further.

So I suggest that you and your board or advisors make this discussion an early and important part of your mutual understanding that will control your philosophy of investing in product or service.

> **Many great products or services have been pushed into the market with a great marketing effort and good salespeople evangelizing a new product into a market that is just not responsive or ready for the offering.**

The Tyranny of the New Office

While we are at it, let's examine a phenomenon I've run into too many times over the years to ignore. New money is injected into a business that is figuratively still in the garage, with people bunched too close together and no extra space for conferences, storage, or privacy. New hires are planned that cannot be accommodated.

So management naturally begins the search for the new facility, worthy of the planned growth over time and in recognition of the inefficiencies of the past environment. Typically, managers seek out facilities more deluxe than the past to show positive movement even if before real evidence of corporate growth. And typically, managers seek space enough for at least three to sometimes five years of projected growth. A new property is identified, a three- to five-year lease signed, and the move made.

The very first day after the move into the new building, everyone marvels at the relative quiet as people spread out into planned spaces. At first, no one notices the level of excitement that drove everyone while in the old spaces seems to have muted into a quiet hum, far less disruptive but far less able to make the adrenaline flow. Then managers begin to fixate upon the empty office space, perfectly planned for future employees, perhaps several years out.

Human nature dictates that empty space be filled. Over time, subtly, employees spread out into corners of space reserved for growth. Equally subtly, new hires seem to come aboard faster than the plan, filling some of that empty cavern. A feeling of satisfaction and growth fills the hearts and minds of senior management. And the overhead just gets bigger and bigger, and the space remaining just evaporates. Slowly, like the frog in the kettle.

> **Human nature dictates that empty space be filled.**

And sometimes, the worst happens. The company needs to move, not because of success into a larger facility, but because of lack of proven success and a resulting downsizing to a smaller facility. And the lease becomes the greatest liability of the company, needing attention to find a sub-lessee or negotiation with the landlord to abate or reduce rent to save the remaining resources of the company just at the worst time.

No one thought about these consequences going in. My theory, developed from years of observation and participation, is that almost every funded company will suffer "the tyranny of the new office" decision by management. And, the nature of small business such that it is, more than half of the new offices leased will end up as a drag upon the dwindling remaining resources of a company just when management needs most to concentrate upon revitalizing the company with limited resources.

My recommendation to all management and boards is to seriously consider the disruption of multiple moves into marginally larger facilities as a strategic decision, accepting the higher multiple move costs and disruptions as a valid hedge against the downside of a large fixed overhead from an unwanted facility in the event of a downsizing.

The other side of this coin is that making the decision to lease the bigger new office is a causal factor in the risk of corporate downfall, not a side effect. Enough said.

Other Monetary Considerations

There is an old rule rarely remembered: Never use short-term money to purchase long-term assets. Invested capital, unless in the form of a short-term note, is long-term by definition. It is contracted for at a cost—in dilution, or interest, or both—as a tool for growth. But short-term bank loans, such as those against receivables or inventory, should never be used to purchase or, if possible, pay down equipment, buildings, mortgages, or even the debt incurred by previous loans from management or the entrepreneurs to the company.

> **Never use short-term money to purchase long-term assets.**

Short-term borrowings must be restricted to working capital needs of a company to avoid future working capital crises.

How about loans from management or the entrepreneur made before funding? Your investors must have a clear knowledge of the terms of each, and together you must find a clear understanding of when and if those loans are to be converted to equity or repaid. Otherwise, the credibility of management is at risk as investors find their funds used for other than corporate growth.

Sometimes the problem works in exactly the opposite way. The company loans management or the entrepreneur cash from its coffers before the funding round, usually because the person has not been paid a living wage or market rate and needs cash for any legitimate purpose. The problem always seems to rise up after funding, in the form of the borrower expecting the loan to be forgiven because of the work done for less-than-market rates or any other good after-the-fact excuse. Again, investors find themselves surprised at the expectation without previous discussion, and react negatively. The entrepreneur or manager, in making the argument for financial forgiveness, is also usually ignorant of the tax effect of the position he or she is in. If a board does agree to forgive any loan, it becomes taxable to the borrower at ordinary income rates, a sure surprise for most all people finding themselves in such a position.

These are just a few of many considerations resulting from funding events that seem endemic in many young companies.

But what of the downside risk? If there are five classes of resources for management to address and control, and if money is the first and most obvious of these, then what about the risk of bankruptcy? And why bring this up first, before discussing all of the positive opportunities to use these forms of resource to reduce the capital drain and extend the runway without cash? Awareness is the key. It is worth the effort to speak to the issue of "keeping enough fuel in the plane," buying a company time to consider, plan for, and use other resources. So we delve into the ultimate risk.

"Running Out of Fuel"—Fiscal Bankruptcy

Here's a story you may recognize from a personal experience of your own. A customer relationship management (CRM) software company, which sold directly into the Fortune 500 international companies, had a big jump on the competition several years ago in their niche, before the dominance of SalesForce, Sugar, and other hosted CRM software, and well before Microsoft polished its CRM system with at least a third release. In other words, management reacted to early success without any consideration for those technologies, more powerful competitors like Microsoft, and even the move toward hosted solutions—all of which were just over the hill but unnoticed by anyone within the firm.

Management celebrated its growing success by finding a new building large enough to "really impress the customers" and handle immediately projected worldwide demand. The problem was that this decision was made as a planned action to accelerate and then handle the challenge of growth. The expected demand would fill their offices with more developers and administrative types, but that growth covered a "hockey stick" spurt expected to take place about two years out. To compound the error, the company's new executive offices were fantastic—truly palatial—in the late European palace tradition; a "Class A" building with a beautiful travertine marble exterior. (Sound like any companies you know?)

Can you guess the outcome, especially after the warning above about the "tyranny of the new office"? In today's market, it is hard to predict demand six months out, let alone two or three years away.

We old-timers may remember the eight-track tape cartridge, invented by Bill Lear of Lear Jet fame. Until arrival of the cassette quickly buried the inferior technology of the eight-track cartridge, it was the darling of the industry (for about a year). What if you had invested in an eight-track manufacturing facility whose demand was for a while outstripping supply? And what if you and your board had decided to build a plant five times the present size to satisfy expected demand over the next three years? You can bring this story forward by substituting cassette facilities with the impending CD over-the-hill or any one of many unseen superior technologies that quickly obsolete those of the most recent past.

In the examples above, company "pilots" opted to build overhead before they built sales—cost push. You can guess that these companies ran out of cash while feeding their newly expanded fixed overhead, and crashed.

There's almost no excuse for running out of cash, but a significant number of businesses do so every day of every business year. The problem is usually not just that there is no more cash in the bank. It is that senior management and the board permitted such blind vision to take their enterprises so far.

> **The problem is usually not just that there is no more cash in the bank. It is that senior management and the board permitted such blind vision to take their enterprises so far.**

So here's a toast to fiscal bankruptcy. May we all plan our way around it, recognize its signs early, and never experience the event itself.

Any pilot, even the captain of a two-seat Cessna 152 trainer, worries about his or her fuel before ever starting the engine(s). You see, pilots do understand that running out of fuel at altitude is a bad thing. Did you know that it's even a violation of a Federal Aviation Administration regulation? (Yes, it is like the government's regulating your business against running out of cash. In some countries, governments do just that.) The important thing to note is that pilots carefully plan with pre-knowledge of the fuel used per hour, the hours necessary to make the flight without wind, and the approximate influence the winds and weather will have upon the duration of the flight. Then, of course, pilots of aircraft *always* obey federal regulations by adding a forty-five-minute or greater fuel reserve, depending upon the type of flight and availability of an alternate airport with adequate weather for a safe landing.

So the question is: How many company managers take the time to create and maintain a realistic cash flow plan using realistic time points for measurement and then track actual expenditures (and actual revenues) against that plan? How fast will revenues grow, month by month, based upon the current product release schedule? How much can the company afford to invest in research for that next product? How many "pilots" are asking—and following up on—these kinds of questions?

There are very few—if our experience is any indication—because very few know how to use such questions to create such a plan, and of those who do, few bother to take the time to work it over or create any reserve for error.

So let's compare the captain of the commercial aircraft to the captain of many a venture-funded company. The former is trained from his or her first ground school session to conserve and manage fuel; the latter usually goes flying by the seat of the pants. The difference in relative approach is worth analysis.

Now I am quick to say that even good aviators can experience a fuel crisis. The weather or winds may require that a pilot deviate from planned course or altitude. Fuel caps have been known to have been misplaced and left off fuel tanks, causing fuel to siphon from the tank into the air stream during flight. And, since there is a maximum weight that can be loaded into the plane, some pilots attempt to cut fuel aggressively to make room for passengers and baggage, hoping for favorable winds en route, or plan to make a fuel stop if there are no favorable winds.

But planning was still the key difference between the two captains (aircraft and business craft) in these examples. And it doesn't have to be…

Of course, there are many alternative sources of cash fuel for today's businesses. And the least amount of preplanning you should do is to acknowledge those sources and be aware of how to find them, analyze their appropriateness to the need, and move to access them if and when needed. Better yet, it would be appropriate to have begun at least preliminary relationships with many such sources.

Without insulting your intelligence, perhaps we should take time out to just list, in order of ease of access, some of those sources—creative financing alternatives to having all the cash you need in the bank.

Cash availability, generally easy for entrepreneurs or managers to get by themselves:

1. Credit cards (so get them before you need them)
2. Slowing down paying suppliers
3. Another home mortgage

4. (Wealthy) relatives (if you were *born* lucky)
5. (Wealthy) friends, partners (if you *get* lucky)
6. Taking on short-term consulting work or projects
7. Entrepreneurial incubators
8. Supporting specialists—intermediaries (*These are people who help find the advanced sources listed further below*)

Advanced sources (*may require the help of supporting specialists—intermediaries*):

1. Finders
2. Deal-packager finders
3. Well-connected attorneys
4. Chief financial officers (hired or "rented")
5. Professional CEOs
6. Advisor-finder-negotiators
7. Venture capitalists
8. Investment bankers
9. Professional restructures

Advanced sources of funds requiring more complex negotiation (*may require experienced specialists on your side*):

1. Prepaid purchases
2. Accelerated payment from customers
3. Prepaid licenses
4. Royalties for specific projects
5. Bank lines of credit
6. Angel investments
7. Strategic partnerships
8. Venture capital investments
9. Pension funds
10. Private placements
11. Public offerings

Now the assumption is that you are reading this because you are part of the infrastructure, either as an entrepreneur, professional C-level executive within a funded company, or an angel or venture capitalist. However, it is amazing to me how rarely management, even experienced management, considers the many alternatives. And of course, there will be restrictive covenants in most every investment agreement and considerations about personal guarantees or liability for management that fall outside of this mere listing of alternatives.

There are many, many options available to the pilot when there is still fuel in the airplane, and very few when the fuel runs out. There is nothing wrong with asking for and getting help in planning, structuring, and creating a sound financial base for the operation. You know you and your business are never quite as attractive as when you don't appear to really *need* the help.

> **There are many, many options available to the pilot when there is still fuel in the airplane, and very few when the fuel runs out.**

Asking for help when the propeller has already stopped and you are gliding to a certain landing is not considered good form. Your options are really clear at that moment, but few. Using the aviation analogy, it is better to declare the emergency while you're still at altitude and the prop is still turning, so that you'll still have enough fuel aboard for guidance to safe harbor.

Financial Insight

Keeping Enough Fuel in the Plane: Avoiding Fiscal Bankruptcy

Assure the flow of adequate capital to meet your requirements. Yes, I know. That's insulting. It's teaching you to fly by telling you, "Successful flying means don't crash the plane."

Does it need to be stated that corporate managers could go a very long way toward avoiding fiscal bankruptcy by practicing planned, long-term capital management? Insight, learned and earned, helps us see the effects of our actions. Using experience, training, and then the question chain ("What if…and then what?"), management can more effectively see into the future, making cash management decisions early, before they become critical emergencies and the available resources are too few to respond effectively.

Money: The Root of all Growth

We have just covered the sources of capital briefly above. So the question that remains is: "Have you identified at least one resource within your board, your advisors, even your management—someone with true financial insight?" That person should be experienced in when and how to prepare a bank loan presentation package and should know how to shop the package and even recognize the elements of a good financing deal from a bad one.

It is also important that you be sure mechanisms are in place to project cash flow on both a long-term and short-term basis. Depending upon immediate runway requirements, this may include a regular thirteen-week rolling forecast and even daily operations summaries. When small, early in the investment cycle, or profitable, a "What's in the bank?" report may do. When large or marginal, much more sophistication is generally needed. But most important, the reports have to be relevant, and they must be read and understood by people with the capacity to modify the company's financial situation.

> **It is also important that you be sure mechanisms are in place to project cash flow on both a long-term and short-term basis.**

Here is a sample format for a thirteen-week rolling forecast you might shape by adding rows to use for your own:

13-Week Cash Flow Forecast

Cash Forecast		6/6	6/13	6/20	6/27	7/4
	Starting cash	68,125	71,252	71,252	111,161	174,020
	Cash in	100,000	125,000	40,972	151,033	108,326
	Cash out	(45,000)	(60,000)	(1,063)	(88,175)	(68,172)
	Payroll	-	(100,000)	-	-	(80,966)
	Net change	55,000	(35,000)	39,909	62,859	(40,811)
	Ending cash	123,125	36,252	111,161	174,020	134,302

(add columns to complete 13 weeks)

After the planning process is completed, to fly the plane effectively, the pilot first keeps the plane *upright*, then assures that the course is set according to plan and that there is enough fuel to make the destination safely. If cash flow is the fuel of business, then you as pilot should be comfortable that you have planned your flight so as to not run out of fuel, and then pay attention to flying the plane.

In aviation, it always means: *first, fly the plane*. Your most recent sales forecasts may reveal an impending order crisis. If so, look for the earliest indicators so you can take cost-cutting action early. Is the pipeline not filling as before—or as predicted within the plan? Are orders running so very high that the company will run out of cash just filling them before collection of the receivables?

Once in the air, fly the plane! Completed business projects or product shipments—when billed—usually result in a short-term increase in cash. Satisfied customers bring in referrals that lead to more satisfied customers. There is no need for an intermediate fuel stop when efficient use of the fuel on board could get you to your destination…

3

It's About Time

"I'm lost, but I'm making record time!" – A pilot, somewhere over the Pacific

"There are two types of airplanes: those you fly and those that fly you… You must have a distinct understanding at the very start as to who is the boss." – Ernest K. Gann

Here's a thought: If we had enough time, we would never run out of runway. Well, time is money and money buys time. The problem with this reasoning is that both time and money are limited resources and tend to run out at the worst possible moment.

We examined money as a resource in the last chapter. But most people do not think of time as an ever-expiring commodity in the business environment. Competitors use time as a weapon to gain ground, create and protect intellectual property or processes, and create brand recognition. Every lost minute is one that can and probably will be used by a competitor to gain ground.

So wasting time is wasting the second most valuable resource you have, other than the cash you raised, borrowed, or earned to grow the business. With that said, this chapter is not about wasting time. It is about deliberately misusing the time of your most valuable resource, defined best as your "bottleneck" resource—the one through which many others manage their schedules. That may be you or your chief developer, production manager, or customer service manager.

In fact, there is a name for deliberately misallocating the time of this bottleneck resource, one I created many years ago to describe this nasty phenomenon. You need to be aware of the time trap, and of tools you need to avoid it and pull your way out of it. Just to make the point, I named this phenomenon "time bankruptcy," and it's time for us to explore its crusty edges.

> **Wasting time is wasting the second most valuable resource you have, other than the cash you raised or borrowed, or earned to grow the business.**

I first noticed what I would later name time bankruptcy during the mid-1970s, shortly after I had entered the computer software industry as an entrepreneur in a new field that was as undisciplined as the old west. My young company's mission—"Create program code about anything and for anyone"—was a bit broad and unfocused. But the computer programming industry was immature, and there was demand for just about every application that could be automated for the first time.

New business was too easy to find. In those days, mini-computer hardware field salespeople would call, introduce me to yet another business entrepreneur with a perceived or actual need for automation of their business, and together the hardware salesperson and I would close the sale in just a few calls. Using a skeleton of an order entry, invoicing, inventory, and accounting program I had originally written for my previous record manufacturing business, I would interview the critical managers of the target business and with less than eight hours of formula questioning, I would have enough information to customize the already-complete program to fit the business. Actual programming changes to the existing code took from two to five working days. My assistants and I worked to make our efforts look like a lot of customization had been done in order to justify our fees, which usually averaged about 10,000 (1970s) dollars for a small amount of incremental customization work.

We could seemingly do no wrong. The business grew from one to five to ten and ultimately to over 230 employees in no time. Looking back, selling my controlling interest in the by-then-public record manufacturing business to get into the new field of computer programming seemed like the wisest decision I had ever made.

More and more often, one of the hardware salesmen I knew would call in a panic, asking us to help him out of a jam he'd gotten into using another, but unfocused, programming house. The stories these salespeople told seemed more and more alike: A software programming company would take a job, promising a large number of customizations, new applications, and special reports. And the delivery would always be short enough of the promised elements to be unusable by the customer, who had almost always given the original programming firm numerous extensions of time to deliver on its promises. Sound a bit familiar? Today, that same flawed role is played out in numerous industries with service enterprises unable to meet their aggressive commitments.

As our fast-rising company was called upon to complete jobs that were abandoned by some of these overcommitted competitors, it became more and more clear to me that the competition was failing to deliver because they had misallocated their most valuable resource—the time of the person leading the team, creating a bottleneck in which all other resources were blocked or useless. Speaking to these entrepreneurs, you'd never know they were in trouble. New cars, new toys, and increasing employee counts were common. It was clear that at this point at least the money was still flowing.

Around that time, I was asked to speak before a number of computer professional and user groups about this disturbing phenomenon. I coined the phrase time bankruptcy to describe it. That phrase seemed to hit a nerve with most everyone who heard it. Years later, people would see me at the COMDEX or Consumer Electronics shows or other industry events and recall me as that time bankruptcy person, often launching into a tale of woe from their own experience.

And some of them used the phrase to describe events and processes in their lives that went far beyond the scope I intended. It seemed that people were finding time bankruptcy an apt description of their condition whenever they felt drained and overcommitted. As we'll see in a moment, the time bankruptcy phenomenon fits into a number of scenarios in business management but is not appropriate for all.

So let me better define time bankruptcy at the outset by contrasting it with that feeling of being overwhelmed that people often described. People can be overwhelmed by demands upon their time coming from external sources as well as by an over-commitment of their own resources. Many times, a person can work his or her way out of overwhelm mode by better delegation, improved time management, and restructuring one's job to exclude some areas of time drainage.

But people who find themselves approaching time bankruptcy do so *because of their own miscalculation; by the conscious or unconscious misappropriation of their own most critical resources.* That can be a big difference.

> **People who find themselves approaching time bankruptcy do so *because of their own miscalculation; by the conscious or unconscious misappropriation of their own most critical core resources.***

If ten new projects arrive at once and your desk is piled high with work to be done, you may well feel overwhelmed. But you will have many choices in dealing with this. You can schedule completion of the new jobs further into the future without too much risk. You can empower others in the organization to perform some of the tasks you would otherwise perform yourself. But in each case, you can dig yourself out of trouble by the application of a little extra effort and better delegation.

Time bankruptcy is far more serious and permanent in the damage it can do to the organization than the overworked environment described above. In a true time bankrupt environment, you or your company's *core resources* will have been overcommitted by you or your staff. Delegation is not an option, since all of your critical resources are already overcommitted. You, as general of your resource army, have committed your troops to battle and have miscalculated the resources necessary to stay in the war, let alone win this battle. The problems created by this action you initiated and the required response by the organization you command are far more serious, difficult to resolve, and a severe threat to the existence of your organization. That's why it has become urgent to focus upon the phenomenon that is time bankruptcy, and to create strategies and tactics to keep us entirely out of this battle, or at least to extract the troops with minimum damage.

First, here is a good example of what is NOT time bankruptcy. You're near the end of one of your typical days. It's 7:30 p.m., and you look at the stack of things to do in front of you that just can't wait. Do you, or don't you?

So you do it again. You pick up the phone and call your spouse/son/daughter/significant other and say those time-honored words: "I've got to finish this work tonight. Put my dinner in the oven. I'll have it when I get home…"

Or: "I can't go to your game this Saturday. I've got so much work piled up I just have to work. I'm sorry—(again)."

We've all done this. The real test is to measure how often and for what reasons. Want to prove it to yourself? Get a pencil and scratch paper. Make the following titles for three columns: "Task," "Hours," and "Percent." Create these task descriptions (and any more that are significant to you):

Task	Hours	Percent
Time with customers—in person		
Customer telephone time		
Meetings with staff		
Informal staff activities (walking around)		
Desk work (administrative)		
Industry upkeep (reading, trade shows)		
Strategic planning, thinking time		
Hands-on research and development		
Drive time		
Other significant time spent	_____	_____
Totals		100%

Spend at least several minutes on this, and don't just skip over the exercise. If you haven't done this before and are honest with yourself, you should be surprised. There is no right or wrong percentage, of course. But it is clear after years of helping hundreds of entrepreneurs and executives think through this same list, that a number of trends emerge. Good managers of well-run businesses spend no less than 20 percent of the time with their customers, no more than 20 percent on desk work, and at least 10 percent isolated in strategic thinking, undisturbed. Although the average work week for managers of young, funded companies falls between sixty and eighty hours, there is time for family or recreation in a balanced business manager's life.

So most weeks, you find yourself thinking, "I did what I thought was right at the time..." or "Why didn't someone tell me they were doing that?" or "Even though this industry's so damned unstable, no one else could have guessed this would happen..."

> **Good managers of well-run businesses spend no less than 20 percent of the time with their customers, no more than 20 percent on desk work, and at least 10 percent isolated in strategic thinking, undisturbed.**

In aviation, we call this *being behind the power curve*. Even though the phrase was created to describe a phenomenon where the aircraft does not have enough reserve power to continue at its present altitude or airspeed, it is often used to describe the above situation where the pilot is thinking slower than the speed of the aircraft. Fast plane, slow pilot: a dangerous combination with a parallel in the business world. That's why this book is written with an "I Learned about Flying from That" flavor, in order to draw some satisfying lessons vicariously from someone else's terrifying and sometimes fatal experience.

Maybe a pilot *can* fly "by the seat of his pants"; and certainly you could run your business in the same way. However, there's an old saying that pilots hear and repeat: *"There are old pilots and bold pilots. But there are no old, bold pilots."*

There are some lessons to be learned from the public companies that have been in the news these past several years for either their prowess or painful fall.

It's About Time

One: Great companies operate with a vision so narrowly focused that most all of us on the outside can explain it with little trouble and in little time. ("Absolutely, positively overnight.")

Two: Management can ruin a good thing without much effort. Companies that were hot last year have disappeared this year, their competitive position and stock value in steep decline. That's a lesson we teach in flying. It's not a very forgiving environment up there. So a course of study leading to a degree in "understanding, reacting, leading, and disaster avoidance" is a very good thing in aviation and perhaps in the business world as well.

> **One:** Great companies operate with a vision so narrowly focused that most all of us on the outside can explain it with little trouble and in little time.
>
> **Two:** Management can ruin a good thing without much effort.

Time Bankruptcy

Running Out of Runway

Here's an aviation story that is retold countless times each winter at airports in many places throughout the world. As you read it, think of how you might respond to the external and internal conditions you observe, and which decision you might make given the circumstances. Here are enough facts to help you make your "go/no go" decision…

The 737's pilot and co-pilot sat motionless in their cockpit seats, still in line for takeoff behind two other "company" planes ahead. All the calculations necessary to assure a safe and legal flight had been completed by the flight planning computer and checked by the pilot. For the weight aboard and at the present temperature, humidity, and runway altitude, this 132,000-pound metal mailing tube should lift off after 4,200 feet of takeoff roll down the 7,000-foot runway. A gentle snowfall had managed to reduce visibility and hamper airport operations, bringing on flight delays and occasional calls for de-icing equipment as planes waited over a half-hour for takeoff.

Snow often melts into water, which freezes into ice when falling upon an aircraft's wings. And as the ice builds, the shape of the wing is altered ever so slightly. Even a half-inch of buildup can alter the wing's smooth upper surface enough to reduce lift by as much as 30 percent, requiring de-icing the wings with alcohol before takeoff.

The plane had been de-iced twenty minutes before, just after push-back from the gate. As the pilots discussed the effect of the ice upon their safety margin, the first of the planes in front of the lengthening line took to the active runway and began its takeoff roll. Both pilots watched silently as the similarly loaded 737 lifted off into the low overcast and disappeared.

A glance out the window at the wings, a look for support toward a cockpit partner, and more minutes of waiting. The only remaining plane in front, a 767, rolled onto the runway and began its takeoff run.

As the second plane lifted into the overcast, the pilot of the now first-in-line 737 seemed lost in his thoughts, staring into his wrist watch. It had now been thirty-two minutes since de-icing. Returning to the gate for another de-icing would merely start the process all over again, as the plane would spend the next half-hour again waiting in line. The snow was light and the wings looked okay. After all, the runway was 7,000 feet long, which normally would accommodate the 737 fully loaded with maximum fuel. The only unknown factor was caused by the small buildup of ice...

Tower cleared the 737 onto the active runway for takeoff, and the co-pilot nodded to his cockpit partner with the understanding that the decision had been made, as the pilot advanced the throttles and began the takeoff roll...

This story is a fictional recount of an event much like that which might happen hundreds of times each day during the winter months. We know from newspaper reports of crashes on takeoff involving icing that the likelihood of a takeoff disaster is remote indeed. In this story, the pilot's dilemma was not easily resolved by either the crew or the airline. In business as in aviation, we'd label this a "gray area" decision, neither right nor wrong. The consequences of a decision to continue ranging from time and money saved and customers not inconvenienced on the one hand to financial and human disaster on the other.

It's About Time

An increasing number of airports are now providing de-icing services nearer the takeoff end of the runway to solve the problem posed above. But we still read of accidents caused by just this icing menace, such as the only-too-true story of the young pilot and co-pilot sitting at the end of the runway in Denver who made the same decision but which became the wrong decision, taking off too long after the application of de-icing, victims of too little experience in their craft. Or the 1992 crash of a US Air jetliner on takeoff from La Guardia that led to the issuing of new regulations by the Federal Aviation Administration regarding wing de-icing procedures.

So with this background, what decision would you have made as pilot in command, knowing the effect of a bad decision? The conservative decision would have been to take this hit, request de-icing again, and assure the subsequent takeoff. The aggressive decision, of course, would probably have resulted in a quick, smooth takeoff and a quickly forgotten challenge. Or maybe not, as in the case of the two Air Florida pilots making exactly that decision without the benefit of combined experience, at what was then Washington National (now Reagan National) Airport on a winter Wednesday in 1982. And that aircraft was a 737, just as the example craft above.

There's a lesson here: Most safety regulations and most regulation of businesses occurs only after a disastrous event where some "pilot" crossed the line of reason or safety.

Professional pilots work from a stringent set of guidelines published by their airlines and approved by the Federal Aviation Administration, all of which govern the decision-making process. Because of demand by the public and authorities for safety margins in the near perfect range, commercial aviation is guided by an overwhelming number of rules to enforce conservative decisions and designed to remove doubt from the decision-making process in the cockpit. Yet who could measure the exact amount of ice slowly accumulating on the wings of that 737 in our story? In the end, the judgment of two pilots determined the decision to accept the takeoff clearance and begin the roll.

In most industries, there is no company guidebook for decision-making; there is no federal approval required before commencing an operation; *there is usually only one captain at the controls.*

Especially in the small to medium businesses segment. Entrepreneurial by its nature, the industry often fosters small, nimble firms headed by a lone decision-maker. The problem is that often the decision-maker has never experienced the problems he or she now faces, does not know where to turn for expert support, and must make decisions without any of the guidelines forced by rules and airlines upon the commercial pilot, that would have assured that he or she addresses the critical safety issues of the company's stakeholders (customers, employees, shareholders).

> **The problem is that often the decision-maker has never experienced the problems he or she now faces, does not know where to turn for expert support...**

The pilots who found themselves in the situation above, in a less structured environment, would have been subjected to any or all of the five dangerous pitfalls we in the business world navigate daily. Yet we can certainly learn from their structured environment as we analyze our business challenges.

As the old salt flight instructor might tell his student: *"Keep the pointy side up and the dirty side down."* It's an old expression that means, "Keep the pointy tail up and the grease stains under the wings...and you'll live to be an old pilot, which by most every measure is a good thing."

Good advice. Learning from aviation, we pay attention to flying the craft above all else; tend to distractions next. Avoid loss of control. That advice works for all of us, no matter what type of craft we fly—or distractions we encounter.

Here's a non-aviation story that illustrates the "loss of control" scenario, one that for the first time focuses in on our definition of time bankruptcy— the deliberate over-commitment of bottleneck resources. This one comes from the enterprise software industry, one filled with such stories.

It's About Time

A new product release, Release 3.0, has been rushed to completion just in time for the annual company users' conference, where the chief technologist for the company (the Wizard) plans to proudly demonstrate it before the attendees as a triumphant climax to the year's development work. Surely, that work includes a number of suggestions made by the users at last year's conference, and all are anxious to see the year's work. The demonstration, given during the first morning's public session, goes very well and everyone basks in the goodwill and feeling of accomplishment.

As a favor to one of the company's larger and most influential users, who asks directly, the Wizard volunteers to install the just-completed software level as a "beta test site" on the user's machine the week following the conference. Eight other power users approach the Wizard during the conference, all with complaints about their present version that could be resolved with the new features and fixes in the new level. As a concession to these eight and in the glow of goodwill enveloping all attending the conference, the Wizard again commits to early beta test installations for five of these, deferring three until general release. (*"The pilot takes to the runway and begins the takeoff roll..."*)

The first test site is installed within two weeks following the conference. The company wisely sends one of its five most senior research and development programmers along with a trainer to "baby sit" the installation. Working fifteen-hour days, the programmer is overwhelmed with changes and fixes to problems discovered by the user under the weight of a live environment. After four intensive days, the programmer leaves, taking with him a list of "to-dos" to complete back at the office. The user is satisfied that his problems are being addressed and puts up with the problems with temporary work-around patches. (*"The plane is 1,000 feet down the runway and gaining speed..."*)

With the fixes made at the first user site safely in the beta "dot two" release, the Wizard bows to pressure created by a tight installer schedule and authorizes the start of the second installation. Telephone support calls from the first user continue to accelerate after the departure of the programmer from the site, and now constitute a noticeable amount of the research and development programmer's time at the home office.

The second installation goes much better without the apparent need for a programmer on site, but the unique nature of the second user's business causes the software to break in new, exciting places. Calls for support are funneled directly to the same research and development programmer at the home office, which he fields along with fixes to the first installation and attempts to keep to his development schedule for other projects as well. (*"Passing 2,000 feet of runway behind, the plane gains momentum and continues its roll..."*)

This process continues through five of the seven sites, with each customer adding new pressures to fix or restore some previously working feature lost in the upgrade. Now the Wizard and programmer are both consumed by the process, spending most of their time on the telephone calming the beta users and fixing code.

By the time the fifth site is due for upgrade, the Wizard-manager realizes the predicament in which he has placed his team. The next beta installation is called off. Almost the total resources of the development and a good part of the support team are now funneled into keeping a lid on the existing problem-plagued beta installations.

When the sales vice president calls the Wizard, asking for a day of his time to make a presentation to a major prospect, the Wizard almost demurs because of the pressures he is getting from the beta sites. But he does agree to go with the sales demonstration, bowing to the constant pressure to write new business. (*"5,000 feet of runway behind... Decision point for aborting the takeoff passing now..."*)

Hold it! Stop (if you can).

What are we doing here? We've allowed someone to "bet the farm" on behalf of our enterprise by pressing a new release into service to satisfy several previously happy super-accounts? Does senior management realize that accepting these beta test installations in rapid succession leads toward an irreversible collision between available time and demands of the marketplace? Would any rational manager place the company in this pressure cooker if they could foresee what forces they would unleash?

It's About Time

The principal problem such a software company faces in the early stages of any new release is the allocation of scarce technical resources. And, in the technology industry, the most scarce resource is the time of the developer or development team. Allocation of that time to put out fires caused by a badly planned, untested, or badly documented new release causes a drain of energy so real and frightening that some hired guns—programmers without a direct financial stake in the outcome—choose to find other work to avoid these unhappy pressures. After all, they had been hired to write exciting new code—not to put out stressful fires.

Any service business can suffer from one of the many forms of time bankruptcy just as easily. See if *this* example strikes close to home…

You commit to a job for Customer One, completing all but the final 20 percent of the work. Both you and your customer recognize that the remaining work will be done soon. The minor inconvenience to the customer is hardly an issue, with goodwill abundantly flowing between you and the customer.

So you move on to Customer Two, obviously needing the money to (fill in the blank) feed the family, pay the payroll, or meet other obligations. Leaving an equal 20 percent of the work left to be done, perhaps because the customer was not ready to absorb the rest of the training or application, among other reasons, you move on to Customer Three. Sometime during that third job, you get a call from your friend, Customer One, gently reminding you that "some work remains to be done." "Be there very soon," you state as you move on to the fourth job, leaving your now-familiar calling card of remaining work to be completed. You start with Customer Four, showing growth in revenues and customer base, happy with yourself for showing such entrepreneurial spirit while having such fun.

Sometime during the fourth job, Customer One calls, disappointment apparent in his voice, and for the first time threatening to withhold from giving out the next positive reference when called by your prospective customers. Just to make your day, Customer Two calls, gently reminding you of your promise to complete the work. With only the best of intentions, you make promises to each that you'll be there shortly to make good. And you move onto Customer Five, because you have to make that payroll or feed the family.

Now Customer One just loses it and, sometime during your work with Customer Five, writes a strong letter threatening suit if the job is not completed immediately. Customer Two, losing patience, calls to announce his unhappy state, as you think, "There goes another good reference." Yes, Customer Three checks in, interrupting your hard and focused work for Customer Five, just to remind you that you promised a visit a while back.

What do you do? Like the rest of us would in the same state, you run not walk back to Customer One and work to complete the job, forgoing any opportunity to even start work with Customer Six or complete work with Customer Five. No new income from this work; it is money already spent or committed. Then it's on to fix Customer Two, again without income. No time to even solicit another job.

Out of money, out of referenceable accounts, out of options, you face the fact that you've failed at this enterprise or at least caused serious damage.

There are many more examples of this frequent occurrence of what we've chosen to call time bankruptcy. This overspending of core, critical, and obviously therefore scarce resources will rapidly damage a company's reputation, perhaps irrevocably. The resulting poor response then drains the goodwill from even the strongest customers, requiring senior management time to patch relationships instead of developing them.

> **Time bankruptcy... This overspending of core, critical, and obviously therefore scarce resources will rapidly damage a company's reputation, perhaps irrevocably. The resulting poor response then drains the goodwill from even the strongest customers, requiring senior management time to patch relationships instead of developing them.**

In the public marketplace, where companies are overseen by boards of directors balanced by members from outside the company, mistakes like

It's About Time

this have caused more than one board to change the company's "pilot" who made such a mistake in judgment.

Another software company I knew had a great product concept and assembled outstanding programmers. Their strategy was to be the first to market with a new communications product. Under the pressure to be there first, they "had to" ignore the quality assurance process. Well, they were first to market. They even were an immediate success.

But then came the support calls. First a few, then hundreds, then enough to overwhelm the company. Their imitators created a similar product with more bulletproof code. While it lacked some of the essential functionality of the originator's product, it worked well. They were never able to develop a second product. When they did decide to overhaul their product, they had to choose between servicing the screaming users or ignoring them and using their resources to create new product. By this time, their reputation was so low among the reviewers, distributors, and dealers that nobody wanted to do business with them.

The conclusion is that quality assurance is always a *pay me now or pay me later* issue, as this company discovered by its blind flying into a mountain of screaming customers.

> **The conclusion is that quality assurance is always a *pay me now or pay me later* issue...**

There's another example of time bankruptcy I've been using for almost twenty years to illustrate the danger. It, too, comes from the technology industry.

A vendor of customized services makes contact with his first customer to modify an existing software accounting package to make it fit the customer's business. Excited to be in a business of his own, the vendor wants to do his very best to create a quality product, deliver quality service, and leave a happy, referenceable customer behind when the job is done. So he bids the job for a fixed fee he knows to be a bit low, but he buys the business with his lower-than-competitive price and sincere promises.

And he goes to work modifying programs, installing the programs at the customer site, and training the employees who will use the system. During this time, his original sales calls have yielded a second prospect that turns into the second customer for a customized installation of the same basic system.

Three weeks into the first installation, our vendor sees that his first company's employee-students have absorbed about all they can for the time being. He makes a short list of things to do, errors to fix, changes requested by the customer, and modules yet to be installed. These collectively amount to just 10 percent of the total job, he estimates as he prepares to move on to the next job. In fact, he is able to collect the full payment from his first customer's president, who sees the results of the job done and is yet unaware of the list outstanding.

Of course, the money from job two looks attractive and by now even necessary to maintain the flow of income. Halfway into the second job, the vendor closes his third sale, using the first customer as a reference.

A repeat of the first experience, the vendor sees the slowing of activity at the second site, makes his list, and prepares to move on pending his return later. A small wrinkle: The president of the second account withholds 10 percent of the price until completion, as called for in the vendor's contract.

Midway through the third installation, the vendor is euphoric. His sales activities are starting to yield many qualified leads, and a fourth contract is signed. He barely took notice when he received the phone call from his first customer's office manager, asking where he was and when he could return to complete the job.

"Next week" was the vendor's obedient reply. And next week came and went as the vendor rushed to complete the third installation so he could be paid the second 50 percent of that contract.

Monday of the following week, the president of the *first* company called, using language more forceful than his office manager and even threatening to give a bad reference to the next prospect who might call. That was enough for the vendor to drop everything and rush to the first account to devote his time, unpaid, to fixing the problems, completing the training, and restoring his bruised reputation.

During which time the *second* company's president called, hinting that he was getting unhappy with the delay in the promised installation and reminding the vendor that he was withholding the remaining 10 percent. "Next week for sure" calmed our fated vendor, aware that the *third* installation was only half complete and half paid, and that the *fourth* had not even begun—even though he needed the money from any of these sources to meet his increasing overhead and living expenses.

This juggling act continued through the first six installations, always with the vendor leaving about 10 percent of the job unfinished as he moved on. With the best of intentions, the vendor found himself at the wrong end of an increasing number of angry phone calls and even his first threat of a lawsuit. Ignoring any new sales opportunities, the vendor found himself completely engulfed in fixing, retraining, offering free time to pacify customers, and making no new revenue-producing contracts in the process.

This poor vendor had allocated all of the time available in putting out fires and working through existing problems, completely unable to focus upon the future.

Time bankruptcy.

Change the nature of the business, and you'll probably recognize yourself somewhere in the last example. *At some time in your recent past, you've probably become time bankrupt without knowing the phrase to describe your predicament.*

Time bankruptcy in a product development environment comes most often from one of four very predictable sources:

1. The product rollout date was committed without a realistic development schedule. The dream won out over the reality (and before the nightmare began).

2. Quality assurance was performed at the customer site after delivery as an expedient move, shortening the delivery cycle but placing the pressure to fix and patch into a live environment. Surely this is more efficient if only one site is involved and the customer willing, but infinitely more dangerous to the customer and the company. (*The best advice for watching a fire is not to get too close. But that's hard to avoid when you're in the plane at 20,000 feet and the fire is in the right wing's only engine.*)

3. Poor planning or poor focus leads the CEO to expect the same speed and quality today that he once achieved with his early entrepreneurial team. There is a failure to calculate the time needed to coordinate and check programmers' work in a larger environment more removed from the chief architect, entrepreneur, or creator of the software. (*It's one thing to change a fouled spark plug in the hanger; and quite another thing to try it at altitude.*)

> **Poor planning or poor focus leads the CEO to expect the same speed and quality today that he once achieved with his early entrepreneurial team.**

4. A bottleneck in the development process reveals itself as the company grows, creating inefficiencies at the other end of the bottle and throwing schedules to the four winds. Simple or complex bottlenecks include funneling all calls through one junior person who is overwhelmed or under-equipped, requiring all production personnel to check with the Wizard before making any changes whatsoever, and having a quality assurance person or group too small or too slow to keep up with the flow of work from the research team.

The issues that lead to time bankruptcy always must be addressed in the early stages. When they become large, they are capable of bringing down even the strongest companies. Just the way that the aircraft is rarely brought down by one bad decision or equipment malfunction, a company usually can develop many signs of an impending crisis before its arrival. And most venture-funded young companies are fragile in structure with limited time in which to find the message, market, and mainstream—amplifying the

It's About Time

pressure to use every available resource effectively, including time and money.

But most entrepreneurs ignore the early warning signs of time bankruptcy, usually out of inability to spot them and assign the right significance to them as they appear. Time bankruptcy is usually at the root of all the other types of bankruptcy we will discuss in this book. Even fiscal bankruptcy is a matter of having too many debts *and too little time* to change the business plan, the product, or just to complete the raising of additional money.

> **The issues that lead to time bankruptcy always must be addressed in the early stages. When they become large, they are capable of bringing down even the strongest companies.**

Retard the throttles on the runway at the first sign of the problem, and you inconvenience the passengers and add a small amount of time to the flight. But then you can safely solve the problem on the ground.

Bow to the pressures of meeting the schedule at all cost, and the cost may prove far greater than the company can pay. Time bankruptcy is generally a result of short-circuiting key processes. It can easily be prevented by analysis, some planning, and a careful scan of the horizon to look for any of the telltale signs.

Earlier, we invoked the old flying truth that *"There are old pilots and bold pilots. But there are no old, bold pilots."* As much as we want to believe that consistent, bold actions lead to bold companies that excel in their respective industries, experience tells another story. The expression about the old and bold pilot tells an unalterable truth.

Bold action is necessary when faced with life-or-death alternatives in which betting the farm may be necessary for survival. And bold action may be entirely appropriate when there is little or nothing to lose, such as in a startup business without large funding requirements. Or it may be appropriate when an emergency situation requires the CEO to step up to the tough decision in a quick, dictatorial move that is at once bold and risky, but unavoidable.

But betting the farm again and again is a sure formula for losing the farm. Flying low and slow as a form of "buzzing" or showing off has killed far too many a young, inexperienced pilot. So the Federal Aviation Administration incorporated a number of rules into its Federal Aviation Regulations, including the rule that no fixed-wing plane fly less than 1,000 feet above populated areas nor within 2,000 feet horizontally from any obstacle in front of the craft, unless on approach to landing. If an inexperienced pilot cannot discern between safety and lunacy, the federal government will do it for them.

Then again, recognize that there are exceptions to the rule. In an emergency, the pilot legally may do anything necessary to regain control of the situation and successfully complete the flight. All he or she need do is explain his or her actions after the fact to the satisfaction of the authorities. Second, in unpopulated areas, when flying less than 700 feet above the ground and with no obstructions in front of the plane, a pilot has only to obey the basic rule that he or she maintain the safety of flight. Therefore, bold maneuvers, within limits, are permitted. The relative danger increases, but not to the level of legal liability.

> **Bold action is necessary when faced with life-or-death alternatives in which betting the farm may be necessary for survival. And bold action may be entirely appropriate when there is little or nothing to lose, such as in a startup business without large funding requirements. Or it may be appropriate when an emergency situation requires the CEO to step up to the tough decision in a quick, dictatorial move that is at once bold and risky, but unavoidable.**
>
> **But betting the farm again and again is a sure formula for losing the farm.**

We think of our heroes in business as bold pioneers who pursued their visions of the future and succeeded perhaps beyond even their own wildest expectations. But within the framework of the flying expression about the old pilots, a closer examination of each bold pioneer will reveal that he or she assumed that role most appropriate for each phase of the flight, and that the bold moves were most often made when there was little to lose, usually early in the life of the company.

Microsoft's Bill Gates very quickly visualized the value of his operating system when given the opportunity to partner with IBM to roll out DOS as a worldwide standard, back when Microsoft was a tiny programming company. But that same Bill Gates has moved many times since then to protect his empire by slowing product releases to ensure quality, and to formalize many business practices required of a large corporation that would have seemed anathema to him a few years earlier. And by moving a bit too boldly and perhaps too hastily, he made decisions for a much larger Microsoft that brought on the unwanted attention of federal regulators and the wrath of millions of users unwilling to accept bugs and security flaws that could have been prevented.

Ray Noorda, who built a networking empire when he acquired Novell, made a career of balancing the bold and conservative alternatives as he acquired complimentary companies and built his empire. But, remember that Novell subsequently fell far behind in the networking race after failing to recognize the importance of emerging trends, and the vast reach of Microsoft into the networking world.

Robert Allen, as president of AT&T, reawakened the sleeping giant during the mid-1990s with massive strategic acquisitions and a number of strategic alliances with creators of new-generation devices and services. And yet Allen fell out of favor with Wall Street for failing to see the significance of the challenges from competitors in a newly deregulated market, and failing to move decisively into the Internet and digital communications revolution, as AT&T fell to become a shadow of its earlier presence, later acquired by one of the spin-off baby Bells who renamed their company AT&T.

Balancing Risk Against Safety

There are three classes of outcome for any business enterprise in balancing risk against safety, ensuring the longest possible ride.

1. *The business could achieve the full potential of its promise* by turning the vision of its founders into a profitable, ever-growing company in a relatively short time.

2. *The business could achieve only part of the potential it might have achieved*, failing to gain the full financial rewards hoped for by the entrepreneurs who founded it. This outcome is very common among entrepreneurs who do not truly understand their target markets or know how to effectively gain full leverage from their resources.

3. *The business could fail (usually from one of the five resource bankruptcies)*. We define failure here either as loss of the investment of money or as the materially unfulfilled vision of management. This is a harsh definition to be sure, since an entrepreneur could have created a business and now continues to simply make a living keeping the business alive and well, but still be classed a failure by these standards of acceptable return upon the entrepreneur's effort, original concept, and/or equity capital.

It's time to comment upon the sometimes-divergent goals between the entrepreneurial team and the venture investor. Venture capitalists aim for a grand-slam home run. They often charge the newly funded company's management with investing boldly toward that goal. Venture capitalists are, as a group, not satisfied with merely profitable, marginally growing businesses. Most would actually rather risk it all in an effort to achieve extraordinary value at the point of an initial public offering or a sale of the company than conservatively manage cash for maximum runway to profitability. This is understandable, given the common venture capitalist profile of backing one major growth company out of every ten investments. However, that same profile recognizes that at least half of the portfolio investments will ultimately fail, with the rest ending up with reasonable returns, perhaps in the two to three times range for the venture capitalist.

It's About Time

So the venture capitalist may, if on the board of the company, tilt the scale toward more risk and less safety, an unbalanced environment for the company. The entrepreneurial team and the venture capitalist need to reach an early agreement as to the balance of risk against safety that the company will endeavor to achieve. Otherwise, the end result is sometimes a full-tilt run toward the end of the runway without liftoff or regard for safety or survival—until the last possible moment when a decreasing number of alternatives remain available to the company's board and management.

Even if such a difference in strategic goal-setting exists early in the investment cycle with the venture capitalist, it is important to speak in advance candidly about when to pull back on the throttles in the event of an increasingly obviously long takeoff roll, in order to preserve the capital remaining to continue what may be a revised business or product plan and takeoff run, or allow time to consider exit opportunities that are not driven by an emergency situation.

For any size of company, reducing the risk is a prudent goal that will give the business more time and more opportunities for a long, successful run. So how do we go about achieving the full business potential from our vision with the least risk? Not by going flying after a pre-flight consisting of just *"kicking the tires and lighting the fires."* There's got to be some skills, some tricks we can use to give us the edge, reducing the risks without making us so conservative that we lose the initiative to make the bold moves.

And there are.

> **For any size of company, reducing the risk is a prudent goal that will give the business more time and more opportunities for a long, successful run.**

We could gain and hone a well-developed *insight* into the mechanisms of resource bankruptcies and use that insight to push our business to its performance limits safely, backing off before we break or bend some metal—damaging the craft, usually prematurely terminating our flight.

Test pilots call this *performing at the edge of the envelope*. And test pilots don't do this lightly, but with preparation, an escape plan to remove them from danger, and a well-developed insight into the probable performance characteristics of the craft—even before they climb aboard. Shouldn't we do the same?

Developing insight means creating the skills to allow us to foresee the effects of an action even before the action is taken. Unlike using a crystal ball to predict the future, developing insight requires calling upon the best of our past experiences and training to help visualize the outcome of a decision in advance.

Insight can come from your cockpit crew's past experiences: *"Don't do it! I did that once and came oh so close to disaster."* Or from your education: *"I remember a case study that covered a situation like this."*

Or insight can come from effective use of the "question chain," a tool you should have in your arsenal to pull out before implementing any major idea. All you need to do is assemble your crew—those members most affected by the outcome of the project—and simply ask: "What if we do commit these resources and are wildly successful (or fail miserably)? And if that happens, what then? So if that's the result, then what? And then? And, after that, what?"

> **Developing insight means creating the skills to allow us to foresee the effects of an action even before the action is taken.**

Following the question chain quickly leads to a vision of the possible outcomes of an action, sometimes revealing the most extreme results of a plan not well conceived, and always leading to a better insight into the alternatives in case things start falling apart rapidly. Your insight can come from your past, the past experiences of someone else who has done it before, your venture capitalist or investor board members, awareness through education, or by effective use of the question chain.

It's About Time

Back to time bankruptcy. It's time for a second visit, this time creating an awareness and insight into things you can do to avoid what we now can recognize as the primary drain upon your scarce resources.

Leveraging Time as a Resource

Never Running Out of Runway: Avoiding Time Bankruptcy

Earlier, I used several stories to explain the gradual, almost unnoticed slide into a deficit of time available for creative use. In the technology company story, the Wizard overcommitted his resources without any insight into the effects of his actions upon the company. Would he have jeopardized the enterprise (as he did) on purpose?

Would you define his risk as calculated?

No, he just screwed up. With all the best intentions of giving his best customers the newly improved product, he succeeded in doing just the opposite and crippling his company in the process. He could have taken the time to create a development and rollout plan, gain consensus from his senior developers as to its likelihood of success, and then challenge his plan with the tool we just defined—the "What could happen next?" management meeting. His insight could have come from the question chain: "If we commit five beta test sites before we've done an adequate job of quality assurance and produced the new documentation, what's the worst that could happen? And then what?"

He could have prioritized his and his department's resources so that strategic requirements such as the need to "create a more competitive version" would be understood to come before tactical opportunities such as "give a special perk to these five major customers." And once prioritized, he could have maintained his leadership role by forcing his group to focus upon the strategic job at hand, avoiding the time drain caused by the pursuit of tactical opportunities out of logical sequence. (Develop, test, document, beta test, release.)

You might call that skill "time insight." If he had it or developed it or found someone with it, he could have easily avoided the problems he encountered.

So when and how does the CEO prioritize his or her time? And what is more important at this stage? Is it the marketing plan? Building a team? Developing a system of values, a corporate culture? Next-round financing alternatives—even preparing for a possible public offering down the road?

No one person can handle all of the elements of creating and growing a business without cutting critical corners. As the company grows, this becomes true of most members of the senior management team as well. With the rapid pace of development in technology, no one individual can know all of what is going on in your industry. A founder who was expert in an area at startup and whose skills the company relies upon for success may become far removed from the new realities of the industry during the process of creating and running a company on a day-to-day basis.

In his 1970 book *Future Shock*, Alvin Toffler predicted that the relatively slow rate of technological change would accelerate beyond imagination within a few decades. Looking back, computer hardware life cycles then were averaging five to seven years. Today, six to eighteen months are all that's generally available for new technologies. Where once it took years to gain market acceptance for new products, now it takes just months.

If we've been around even a short time, we've surely been guilty of missing the mark in guessing the movements of our own industry's market.

And that's the *good* news.

We've surely been guilty of missing the mark in guessing the movements of our own industry's market.

And that's the *good* news.

The bad news is that competitors also move much more quickly than they did in the past in bringing their competitive products to market. Worse, without rapid effective product modifications, any product or service can become quickly obsolete, forced into early obsolescence by the competitor's next generation or a new and improved version of your own product. The result is an increasingly narrow product window, requiring introducers of new products and services to move quickly in getting effective market coverage and penetration.

So we introduce *time leverage*.

If you have the right internal *company* infrastructure to effectively move quickly with your strategic plan, and if you have divined the correct stage of maturity and development within your *industry* to position your company optimally, then you have *time leverage*.

Properly leveraging your time means your company is positioned to move faster than your competition, which is often the difference between success and failure in a world with short product life cycles and agile competition.

Time bankruptcy can be avoided by effectively leveraging available time by:

- Doing only the strategic things first
- Outsourcing non-core components of the job
- Making use of just the right tools and resources to reduce the total time required

A CEO who is expert in doing these things is an artist and should be valued for his or her skills and emulated at every opportunity.

Time is like an unoccupied airline seat or hotel room. If not used, it is lost forever.

With enough time, almost any problem can be solved as long as the problem does not boil over while the solution is cooking. The trick is to reduce the amount of time required to do any job well—forcing your competition to follow your agile lead. Time bankruptcy is the result of poor allocation of this unrecoverable resource and a lack of insight as to the outcome, as the process takes its inevitable toll.

> **Time is like an unoccupied airline seat or hotel room. If not used, it is lost forever.**

4

Management of Relationships

"Nothing is impossible for the person who doesn't have to do it (all) himself." – AH Weiler

The third of our points of focus is upon your golden Rolodex of relationships to help you more quickly achieve your objective, reducing cost and improving speed to market.

Everyone in your management team has some depth of personal and professional relationships from which to cull advice and find additional resources. This you will find to be especially true in members of your board. If you have done a good job of creating a viable board, you will have at least several industry professionals available to you who have done this before, and who have a deep list of friends and acquaintances at their command to help you and the company. One of the most important benefits of accepting venture funds has nothing to do with the money and everything to do with the relationships your new venture capital partner brings to the table.

In this chapter, we will analyze the importance of relationships in the success of your enterprise and in providing new resources to extend your runway. Let's first review the story of the first solo flight across the Atlantic Ocean, an amazing feat in 1927, and how relationships made that flight possible.

"Lindbergh Flew It Alone, Too!"—Relationship Bankruptcy

Charles A. Lindbergh piloted the first aircraft to fly the Atlantic Ocean, non-stop between New York and Paris in May of 1927. This was a most remarkable feat at the time and captured the imagination of the entire world during and after the thirty-three-hour trip over water. Accorded the status of world hero, Lindbergh was received by heads of state in Europe and by the president of the United States. The city of New York went wild upon his return, according him a ticker-tape parade unlike any ever seen before that time.

All for a major accomplishment in an industry that was then just twenty-four years old, dating just from the Wright brothers' historic flights in 1903.

Who has defined the modern vision and standards in your industry? Who is the Lindbergh that made your industry into a celebrated marketplace—as Lindbergh focused the world's attention upon aviation? In the micro-computer and software world, Bill Gates is the first name that comes to most minds. Gates made his deal with IBM to supply to them the DOS operating system that started the revolution in 1981. At that time, Gates was a year older than Charles Lindbergh was in 1927 when he flew the Atlantic. Add the stories of Marc Andreessen, who with his small cadre of developers made the Web accessible to the masses, or of Sergey Brin and Larry Page, two Stanford students who made searching a science and enhanced our abilities to make sense of the billions of pages of data available. These three stories tell of entrepreneurs who enhanced existing industries and created entirely new sub-industries as a result.

Technology as an industry has experienced considerable growth over the last decade. The Internet is responsible for much of this, as access to the largest network on Earth has become a birthright for citizens of the world.

The energy industry took center stage shortly after the turn of this new century and shows no signs of becoming less than a primary driver of inflation and a continued threat to world growth. Nothing remains constant, and it's a sure bet that the next industry to take the stage will be driven by entrepreneurs with singular visions, using all the resources available to achieve their goals and relying upon relationships to fund,

Management of Relationships

develop, and market their products. Although we speak of technology-driven industries almost exclusively in this book, the next drivers will probably be driven by biology, and bio-sciences use technology and chemistry to develop new frontiers for new business opportunities well into this century.

Put this into perspective. The aircraft industry began its tremendous growth period back in 1939; the Internet in 1995. Are you at the knee of the curve in your segment or industry? Is there a product or service you've identified that will accelerate your industry into the center stage? Knowing that these overarching opportunities come along perhaps once in a generation, you must keep your antennae up for the chance to ride these waves when they arrive, a preview of the chapter to follow dealing with "context."

But back to Lindbergh.

Actually, Lindbergh didn't fly the Atlantic alone. That's the point. Charles "Slim" Lindbergh was a young daredevil parachute jumper who borrowed $500 in 1923 to buy an Army surplus Curtis "Jenny" and taught himself to fly. He later became a flying cadet in the Army and then a mail pilot working for Frank Lambert, owner of a flying field in St. Louis, Missouri.

It was during one of those monotonous nighttime mail flights between St. Louis and Chicago that Lindbergh claimed he "got the idea that he was the one who would be first to fly from New York to Paris." In 1926, a Frenchman, Raymond Orteig, offered a prize of $25,000 to the first person or group of flyers who would attempt to fly solo in a heavier-than-air aircraft (excluding blimps) between the two cities, separated by the Atlantic Ocean—a feat considered too dangerous for the aircraft and airmen of the time.

Convinced that with the proper plane (which he would help design) he could make that flight and make it alone in the cockpit (unlike all the others, who were planning to fly heavier planes for the prize with multiple pilots on board), Lindbergh became his own promoter. Early on, Lindbergh asked Frank Lambert, with whom he'd developed an excellent relationship and who had a fine reputation in St. Louis, to help him find the capital and other resources he would need to achieve his objective. Lambert contacted a number of prominent St. Louis businessmen and helped Lindbergh sell the concept of a flight in the *Spirit of St. Louis* to promote the city. Lindbergh, to show his confidence in the venture, besides risking his life, put up $2,000 of his own money. Lambert then invested and helped him raise a total of $15,000 from three other businessmen friends and himself.

In February of 1927, Lindbergh entered into what today would be called a "strategic partnership" with the Ryan Aircraft Company of San Diego, California, to build the plane he envisioned. Ryan was the only company willing to meet Lindbergh's deadlines and price. The Wright Aeronautical Company supplied the engine, and others created special equipment to make the plane fly faster with the lightest weight possible.

And at 7:54 a.m. on the morning of May 20, 1927, Charles Augustus Lindbergh barely cleared the telephone wires at the end of muddy Roosevelt Field in New York, inching into the air carrying 5,250 pounds of weight, 1,000 pounds over the design gross weight of the airplane. And 3,600 miles and 33.5 hours later, Lindbergh landed at Le Bourget Airdrome in Paris, almost missing the field as he approached it in the dark at 10:24 p.m. Paris time.

Did Lindbergh fly the Atlantic alone? Not even close. Lindbergh was the entrepreneur of a venture that required:

- A vision: *"I can fly from New York to Paris, alone."*
- A goal: *"I can do it first—and win that $25,000 prize."*
- A financing plan: *"I'll sell my vision to these city fathers."*
- A strategic partner: *"I'll help Ryan create an airplane for the task."*
- A plan with strategies and tactics: *a carefully mapped flight log and plan*
- Execution of the plan: *hourly position checks with course corrections*

Any of the elements in the Lindbergh chain, if defective or under-attended to, could have easily brought the fragile project down.

Lindbergh succeeded because he used his vision to excite others into developing relationships with him and with those who would support his efforts. The city fathers would not have supplied the cash if they had not

Management of Relationships 83

known, respected, and believed in this enthusiastic and talented entrepreneur. Ryan would not have dedicated his entire aircraft factory, including design engineers, to a project that would make no profit and could have failed making the worst possible publicity outcome for the small manufacturing company. Conversely, Ryan bought the vision and developed a trusting relationship with the person who could and later did make an international reputation for the tiny company. Others who designed special equipment for this special flight would not have risked their reputations and time if they, too, had not been caught up in the excitement.

In the business universe, sound and competent relationships are required to bridge the wide gap between vision and achievement of the goal. The most successful companies have been those where competent relationship partners were recruited to help fill the gaps required in the execution of the vision. And interestingly enough, often it is the same individuals who combine again and again to form strategic relationships for new ventures, based upon the comfort each partner took from the preceding venture.

> **In the business universe, sound and competent relationships are required to bridge the wide gap between vision and achievement of the goal. The most successful companies have been those where competent relationship partners were recruited to help fill the gaps required in the execution of the vision.**

Even in the venture capital world, the businesses funded are often financed because of relationships, not business plans. How many startup companies do you know that developed a complete business plan and were funded as a direct result of mailing the plan to a number of venture capital firms? My venture capitalist friends have often told me they would always look at a plan generated by people they know and respected, even if the initial plan was just scribbled on a table napkin.

Knowing the entrepreneur or his or her advocate has been a far greater factor in positive venture funding decisions than any other single decision-making criteria over the years.

But following funding, ventures need to attract the most competent marketing, development, and managerial talent possible to rise above the noise created by the hundreds of similar ventures competing for the attention of distributors, dealers, and customers. Competent management teams make superior businesses possible.

Conversely, an entrepreneur's style of "going it alone" has killed more opportunities in the long run than almost any other force by serving to drive away competent help.

To fly it alone is not a viable option in today's business world. The next time someone uses Lindbergh's flight to illustrate how one person can do it all alone, remember the full story. And understand that failing to develop relationships can lead to a venture that dies from more obvious external causes underpinned by the larger failure to build competent relationships with those who could have prevented failure, encouraged growth, and added value to the business.

"Relationship bankruptcy" is the name we've given this lone eagle syndrome.

> **Conversely, an entrepreneur's style of "going it alone" has killed more opportunities in the long run than almost any other force by serving to drive away competent help.**

Relationship Insight: Relationship Leverage

Remembering That Lindbergh Wasn't Alone: Resisting Relationship Bankruptcy

Lindbergh could never have flown the Atlantic alone in 1927. But many of us try a similar feat all of the time. But remember that Lindbergh had a goal,

Management of Relationships

a plan to reach that goal, financing to fuel the plan, strategies and tactics to support the plan, and strategic partners at most every point except the hours in the air.

Relationships multiply our effectiveness and help us reach our goal with someone else filling the gaps in our resource needs. Why would such giants as Microsoft and NBC join together to form a joint venture in the broadcast arena combining the Internet and television if each thought themselves capable of executing a project alone? In our current complex business world, even the biggest players need help in coming to market faster with less risk and a better product. Relationships between technology companies such as Microsoft and content providers such as Disney are commonplace and growing at an astounding pace. There is not one multimedia enterprise targeting the home entertainment mass delivery market that has chosen to do it alone. Those with the movie titles need a delivery tool; those with cable satellite or telephone assets need software and media. Such opportunities for alliances exist at all levels of business.

But there are other, more direct types of relationships that are absolutely vital to the growth of every business. These include relationships with key customers, employees, distribution and marketing groups, backup talent for current management—along with venture capital and other funding sources, and potential strategic partners.

> **Relationships multiply our effectiveness and help us reach our goal with someone else filling the gaps in our resource needs.**

Without a banking relationship, few businesses can grow into the international marketplace or cover short-term financial needs.

Without strong customer relationships, a company cannot exploit customer goodwill to achieve solid market acceptance, ensure customer support for changes in company direction, or mount a successful public relations campaign based upon customer success stories.

Without key long-term funding relationships, a company cannot consider plans for financing long-term growth from anything but working capital or additional contributions from current investors.

And without strong key contacts in other areas of your resource limitations, you generally cannot grow to reach your full potential. So by now, you should have gained an overwhelming sense that most companies are in a marketplace that requires that management seek all the assistance it can find and afford in order to overcome market pressures, competition, financial challenges, and organizational inefficiencies.

Building strong relationships relatively quickly in time of need requires *relationship insights* to know who, what, when, where, and how to find needed resources. But it generally also requires strong contacts and good credibility, or *relationship leverage*.

> **Most companies are in a marketplace that requires that management seek all the assistance it can find and afford in order to overcome market pressures, competition, financial challenges, and organizational inefficiencies.**

How do you find, identify, and gain access to resource leverage? The keys are having a broad understanding of your industry and company, and having personal creditability. The need for broad understanding is what drives the venture capitalist to require a reasonably detailed but broad business plan, then follow it up with formal due diligence. It's also why the best of them conduct extensive informal due diligence, or deal again and again with people they already know and trust. A venture or resource professional would express it this way: "If I haven't taken the time to know you well enough to really understand what you're saying and 'where you're coming from,' how am I going to evaluate what you report—and provide feedback you'll appreciate and act upon?"

"Most importantly," the venture capitalist might continue, "if I don't really know you and understand the situation you're in, how can I risk my hard-earned creditability by getting others to take major risks in working with

Management of Relationships

you? And if I don't have an understanding of your business, or creditability with the resource I know, why do you think I'd be able to help you with relationships quickly in high-risk situations?"

In the aviation world, management (the pilot) is required to undergo recurrent training and even recurring skills and knowledge testing to remain current and legally able to fly passengers. In turn, passengers trust their lives to the pilot with the assurance that the pilot understands what is happening and can be counted upon to act prudently. There is no equivalent government decree for the business world. (Well, there is the prospectus for a public offering, and it only defines the situation of the business and the track record of the principles, not their competence.)

We certainly would not want any more government interference at the strategic and operational level in the name of shareholder protection. We are going to feel the long term impact of the Sarbanes Oxley Act for the indefinite future. Regulations will only increase over time. Can you think of any business regulation that has been eliminated during the past decade?

Yet it would be extremely beneficial to the company if management could find high-level help to leverage their use of available time, tighten their focus, and aid them in carrying out their goals. It would be much like a *flight instructor* within the business world.

A flight instructor who, as an expert, can help management hone their skills, focus their attention upon safely flying the plane, and who can use his or her insight and leverage to help find those resources needed to safely navigate the craft, avoiding the five resource bankruptcies we now know so well and perhaps dread so much.

Luckily, such people are generally available. Sources include members of your board including venture capitalists, industry friends who will act as advisors to the business, pools of retired executives interested in keeping a hand in the business world part-time, consultants who have run larger companies within the industry, and a new emerging group of hybrids who call themselves "active angels." The latter early investors often willingly coach senior management and take board-level positions. Some work for stock options or charge consulting fees.

There are also networking associations made up of professional facilitators who bring together key executives from similar businesses to discuss common problems and help bring solutions to unique problems brought to the group by its members.

One of the best such industry groups—the ABL Organization—is an organization of senior technology executives in Southern California. Bob Kelley, advisor for this book, is the CEO of that organization, while I act as its volunteer chairman of the advisory board. Over the years, we've participated together in well over 1,000 roundtables with hundreds of senior executives from diverse companies, all with problems often in common. Using the roundtable format, meeting monthly year after year, members grow to trust their peers, often revealing problems they have not shared even with their own boards or other senior managers in order to find solutions or role play outcomes. Employee, business partner, board, financing, growth, and legal problems are discussed freely in an atmosphere of confidentiality and trust. Any reasonable membership charge for such valuable advice from one's peers in a structured environment is worth the paying.

Relationships are everything. (I said that about vision, too, but you can forgive the enthusiasm in the name of making an important point.) The culture of your enterprise is more a reflection of the relationship-building actions of the CEO and senior management than any other single factor. Relationships define the personality and often the success or failure of the enterprise. And yet it is this aspect of enterprise development that is most often underrated or ignored.

> **The culture of your enterprise is more a reflection of the relationship-building actions of the CEO and senior management than any other single factor. Relationships define the personality and often the success or failure of the enterprise.**

5

Process Management

"I never did anything worth doing by accident, nor did any of my inventions come by accident. They came by work." – Thomas A. Edison

"Stupid is as stupid does." – Forrest Gump

One of the benefits of finding experienced managers is that they know the process of building a company, creating a product or service, and managing through a series of expected and unexpected crises to achieve a goal. Conversely, enthusiasm alone cannot overcome a deficit of process knowledge without cost, either in money or in time.

It would seem to be easy to define the processes for completion of tasks to achieve a business goal. But as we will learn in this chapter, there are many ways to navigate from start to finish, some fraught with unseen perils.

Such as the *every $3 million crisis*. It's a phrase I created years ago to describe another phenomenon I observe regularly in growing businesses, especially in their early stages.

The Every $3 Million Crisis

See if this story rings even a little bit true for you and your past experience. Three good buddies who have worked successfully together agree to start a new business, each contributing equally their knowledge and equal initial capital to fund the business. Early on, no outside capital is needed, as the three partner-investors begin to work on growing their business. Their service company offering seems just right for their initial market, and initially customers who are familiar and comfortable with the founders are easy to find and serve.

Charging a bit less than the competition, the three have agreed that they will start by competing principally on price until their reputation is secure and they can raise prices. That tact works well for the three—that is until the volume of business reaches the capacity of the two who agreed to work outside the office with the customers and no new business can be taken until a new employee is brought on. With barely any remaining cash after paying the living costs of the three, the partners failed to realize that multiple problems were gaining upon their small enterprise. For example, receivables had grown to a point where working capital was needed to cover operations until customers paid for services rendered in the near past.

Bills began to pile up as the in-house partner, acting as bookkeeper, waited for cash receipts in order to make payments. More growth, more working capital needs. Calls came in from vendors with overdue bills, first slowly then at an alarming rate.

The first crisis for this fragile enterprise turned out to be one of quickly needing to identify and secure sources of working capital—a financial crisis. And none of the three knew where to start. With time, they contacted their local bank, agreed to personally guarantee a line of credit, and overcame the first crisis. Meanwhile, the newly hired employee needed much more handholding than the field partners had time to give without cutting into their own billable time. As a result, the new employee was not productive to the level of the others. Nor did his quality of his work measure up to the standard set by the three as they set out to conquer the world. Service quality, never an early problem, became one to recon with and quickly solve. So the second crisis turned out to be one of product/service quality.

Another new employee was soon needed, and it became clear to the partners that none of them had time to manage two and soon more technicians in the field, and that even with their meager working capital, a new manager was needed, or one of the two field partners would have to come in out of the field in order to scale this business. The third crisis was one of organization, typical of such small enterprises.

Process Management

The partner back in the office, handling the office and accounting duties, proved unable to handle the accounting and office workload, having little experience with this now-distasteful activity he was only marginally equipped to perform. The other two partners, working long and productive hours in the field, began to openly question the inside partner's relative contribution to the company, wondering aloud whether it was time to gently nudge him out of the organization—a management/ownership crisis.

As the company grew further, the now relatively small bank line proved to be inadequate for immediate needs and projected growth—a second financial crisis in the brewing.

Well, you get the idea. A continual series of rotating crises—in this case financial, quality, organizational, ownership, and in circular fashion back to financial—all seemed to occur at intervals in the development and growth of the young enterprise.

The question for you is: Why not identify these predictable crises early and move aggressively to mitigate their damage to the enterprise?

In my earlier software business, I noted that these crises seems to occur at every $3 million of increased revenue, enough to represent the addition of about fifteen or twenty new employees, and that these crises did rotate from one type to another in a semi-orderly fashion. After years, my growing management team and I noted the regularity with which these occurred and that we'd all be more comfortable at executive meetings focusing on growing signs of the next crisis, attempting to solve these coming problems in an orderly, non-disruptive fashion before they erupted into full-fledged crises.

As we grew through the $25 million revenue level and over 200 employees, we felt more confident as a senior leadership team that we were able to identify these and put solutions in place before damage was done to the culture or fabric of the enterprise. By the way, although the $3 million level

> **The question for you is: Why not identify these predictable crises early and move aggressively to mitigate their damage to the enterprise?**

is entirely subjective, we continued to note the regularity of these events. Our example above dealt with a much smaller enterprise in an earlier stage of its growth, but the fact of the rotating crisis is not diminished but rather amplified by enterprise size.

We needed to recognize that the process needs to accommodate for growth and change accordingly to fit the enterprise at the moment. We knew solutions that fit yesterday would be stretched until broken and require new solutions to coming problems in the future—all connected with the process of moving a company from initial organization through reaching its goals.

> **Solutions that fit yesterday would be stretched until broken and require new solutions to coming problems in the future—all connected with the process of moving a company from initial organization through reaching its goals.**

Time and Process Interlinked

Almost no one correctly estimates the time it takes to get a new senior employee or manager up to speed. Here, thanks to an old friend and fellow CEO roundtable member, Dick Tanaka, is a startling theory:

> *It takes eighteen months to replace a senior-level manager from the time you first identify that the person is not a good fit until the replacement is fully functional.*

Eighteen months? A company can interview and hire within a month or two at most, you'd respond. Dick points out that we need to recalibrate the problem, taking into account the complete process for replacing someone with critical responsibilities. His argument goes something like this…

In June, you begin to notice that Stanley, your director of research and development, isn't managing his people well and often seems impatient with the customers who appeal to him when problems are not fixed by those in support. So you speak with Stan, frankly expressing your concerns, which you've now heard directly from some of your best customers. Stan promises to do better and handle his customer calls with more finesse. You also mention that his direct reports seem less productive than expected, noting that the project reports show his department falling further behind each month.

By early August, you note no measurable improvement in Stan's behavior or management skills, and you call him in again for a talk. This time, you develop a ninety-day plan to measure improvement, agreeing together on the elements of the plan and ending the meeting with a feeling that with metrics in place, this might work.

Come early November, you meet as scheduled with Stan to review the plan and metrics, and you find him deficient in both areas of measure. Reluctantly, you give him a thirty-day notice to improve or be let go, and place a written notice in his file as required by your process.

Mid-December comes; you are now convinced that Stan must go. But it's the holiday season, and you let the issue slide through the first week of January, when you call Stan in and gently give him the axe. In this instance, as is typical in such events, you offer severance in return for Stan's signing of a release, and Stan departs that day forever.

You start the search process by interviewing several search firms, rightly thinking this is too important a position to trust chance or networking to find a replacement for Stan. By mid-February, you contract with the search consultant and begin the process of writing the job specification and publishing it through the search firm. By mid-March, you are ready to interview the top three or four candidates presented by the search firm and have the candidates in turn be interviewed by other of your managers and even a selected number of future direct reports.

April 15, you select the finalist and begin the negotiations. May 1, she accepts the position, starting June 1, allowing for notice to her present employer.

The next six months fly by as your new research and development manager comes up to speed, arriving by early December at a level of corporate and product understanding that allows you to be fully confident that your new find can now do all Stan could, know all Stan knew, and perform his job as expected when hired. Eighteen months.

Sure, that amount of time to get a critical new hire up to speed could be shorter—but after reviewing the process described above—much, much longer than you would have originally estimated. That's the point. The time to fully engage in a complex process is almost always longer than originally estimated.

Where or Who Is the Bottleneck?

While we're at it, here is the next process consideration to examine in attempting to identify hidden causes for eating into resources over time—the bottleneck.

Remember the Wizard in the example of time bankruptcy earlier? The Wizard was a bottleneck through which all research and production processes had to pass. And he was ultimately consumed by the flow of events to the point where he was ineffective at all of his various job responsibilities.

Every business has one or many bottlenecks preventing a smooth flow of production and most efficient use of resources. Often, that bottleneck is the boss. If every decision beyond the most elementary ones must be run by the boss, if people line up at the boss's door, if the boss needs to tell any direct report consistently that he or she will be back with comments or a decision in the morning—that boss is the first and most critical bottleneck. It is a sure sign that the process steps to complete a piece of work or a project run through the boss's office—no matter at what level that person is within the organization chart.

> **Every business has one or many bottlenecks preventing a smooth flow of production and most efficient use of resources. Often that bottleneck is the boss.**

Process Management

One of the most respected books in the manufacturing world is Eliyahu Goldratt's *The Goal: The Process of Ongoing Improvement*. I have found that this book, written to deal with manufacturing process bottlenecks, has been the best ever written to describe bottlenecks in a new light as they could apply to any resource from machines to people, in any industry from manufacturing to software production. I strongly recommend that if you have not read this book, you read it and share it with your contemporary managers in a dedicated planning session that looks for and removes bottlenecks throughout your organization. You'll be amazed that, once you embrace the concept that any enterprise can and does suffer from critical bottlenecks in process, you will be able to identify and solve numerous problems that will free your enterprise to work measurably more efficiently.

I now require that each of the CEOs with whom I work as board member or chairman read *The Goal*, and that we hold a management planning session dedicated to the task of breaking bottlenecks. It's rewarding in so many ways, and virtually cost-free at that.

You'll know the answer to the next question before I can fully ask it. So what would we call the deficiency in process knowledge at the management level in an organization? Of course, *Process bankruptcy*. Let's explore the dark side of process knowledge.

"The Navigation Nightmare"—Process Bankruptcy

We've chosen the flying metaphor for use in this book because it seems so simple. In comparison to the chaos within the business world, flying is so…precise. Take for example the creation and filing of a flight plan. Using the known airspeeds of your aircraft at various altitudes, knowing the exact route of flight from Point A to Point B, and automatically downloading into your flight-planning PC the winds aloft for the route of flight from the National Weather Service computer, it is a simple matter for a PC software program to plan an exact flight plan, select the most appropriate altitude, calculate the fuel required, print the resulting plan, and even automatically file the flight plan with the Federal Aviation Administration.

Planning a flight, filing the flight plan, and then actually flying the plan to arrive safely at the destination constitute a process. Pilots of all classes and skill levels know and use the process repetitively before each cross-country flight. Failure to perform any of the parts of the process would add unnecessary risk to the flight. Failure to fly the plan often exposes the pilot to a chance of never, ever arriving at the intended destination.

There are defined pathways between each process that are easy to comprehend and follow. A pilot knows where to get weather information, what to do with it, where to find route information, and how to plan and fly to his or her destination.

But what if the pilot knew only *that* he needed to get from Point A to Point B, and nothing of the processes required to get there? Or worse yet, what if he knew he was at Point A and wanted to be somewhere else—anywhere else.

That's what many of our friends who've started businesses have done, even if inadvertently. For example, take Doug, who is the author of a software package for automating delivery routing for trucks. Developed as an in-house solution for one company and paid for by the customer company, the "package" Doug developed lacked documentation and had never been installed at another firm to test the universality of the solution. Doug knew he had a solution that had worked at his own firm and that he wanted to market the package. And that's about all.

At this point, Doug lacked knowledge of the process, had no clear goal, and had no understanding of the pathways to travel to achieve the unknown goal. What were the odds of his success?

The truth is that the odds were unknown. The product might have had universal appeal to a large number of customers who would pay for and implement the package internally, unlikely as this would be in today's mature vertical software marketplace.

But Doug's example serves to point out the need to understand the process and define the goal itself. A clear goal for an enterprise is not the same as a mission statement, which defines the overall company's reason for being. A goal defines Point B as in: "Grow the company to $5 million in revenue with at least 10 percent profitability within three years." Such a clearly

Process Management

stated goal begs for the creation of pathways made up of strategies and tactics designed to achieve the goal, and metrics to measure progress. Together they form the map to Point B so that you'll at least know when you've arrived.

Pathways to achieve a goal lead from Point A, where you are today, to many waypoints or milestones advancing in the direction of Point B. The company's strategies define the direction and distance of the pathways. Perhaps the goal is not attainable without a strategic alliance with a partner with some required element of the enterprise, such as manufacturing facilities, a training and support infrastructure, a distribution channel, marketing expertise, or funds to finance the effort.

If Doug were completely unaware of the steps necessary to build an infrastructure to support his development, product marketing, installation support, and corporate administrative requirements, he probably could not execute a plan even if he had one.

We've seen many an entrepreneur with a newly developed product for the retail marketplace with no clue of what to do with it. They may be unaware of what it takes to produce, package, and release a product through broad distribution channels. They may be unaware of the costs and steps necessary to launch a campaign to prepare the market for the product; unaware of the infrastructure necessary to transition from an idea into a professionally led enterprise. Any positional unawareness of this kind can easily doom an entrepreneur with even the best idea or product.

Building the infrastructure is part of the process of getting from Point A to Point B and achieving the goal. Starting out in business with an idea at Point A and little else is a sure step toward getting lost somewhere between Point A and nowhere. Lost because of failure to define a process, a goal, strategies to achieve the goal, and metrics to measure progress along the way.

...A candidate for process bankruptcy.

One way to achieve the goal without knowing the process itself is to make a strategic relationship deal with someone who has the infrastructure and knowledge. So you can say that making good deals is often a key to sound, rapid growth.

Many product inventors or developers enter into exclusive contracts with larger companies who have established distribution, only to see the larger company fail to put any real effort into marketing the product or—worse—deliberately leaving the product on the shelf to avoid competing with an existing or planned "knock-off" internal product.

In one recent case, a developer licensed a product to a large company at an acceptable 12 percent royalty based upon the price the larger company planned to charge for the product. When the product was finally introduced, the larger company unilaterally decided upon a much lower price, reducing the royalty to an unacceptable level without the developer's consent.

Either way, the distributor wins, all because the developer was not equipped to handle the negotiation or fully aware of the meaning of all the terms of the agreement.

So all of these examples lead to the need to understand, develop, and control the infrastructure necessary to achieve the goal. These examples also lead to the clear picture the entrepreneur or business manager needs to develop the pathways and protocols to tie into their infrastructure those who can help the enterprise with the essential six elements of knowing—who, what, how, when, where, and why—necessary in understanding how to direct a company toward and achieve a goal.

Conversely, failure to develop such critical processes and form such an enterprise infrastructure could be defined as process bankruptcy, as the net result could be failure of the business itself. The *who, what, how, when, where, and why* knowledge elements form the waypoints in the navigation map to a successful enterprise. Without them, there would be no clear way to find your destination, even with the map in your hands as you fly, because it will be hidden somewhere among the clutter at the other side of the map.

The six points of process knowledge above are like six required waypoints on the map. Lose sight of just one, and the course line just disappears. All must be clearly identified in order to avoid the "navigation nightmare" and navigate the complete flight safely.

> **Failure to develop such critical processes and form such an enterprise infrastructure could be defined as process bankruptcy, as the net result could be the failure of the business itself.**

Process Insight!

Planning Our Way Around the Navigation Nightmare: Sidestepping Process Bankruptcy

Getting from Point A to Point B is a process. There are probably lots of ways to do it, but only a few highly efficient ways. But many times, businesses develop highly convoluted flows and paper trails and compartmentalized operations that not only inhibit the achievement of the goal (get to Point B), but obscure the goal entirely (serve the customer).

Businesses everywhere are rethinking the processes they have built to achieve their goals. It's a matter of focus upon analyzing the way you carry out the development, production, distribution, and accounting for your products and services. One key question you should ask: "Is anyone complaining about slow or inefficient operations of the company, especially a customer?" If so, examine your process of delivering the problem product or service to find bottlenecks like the kind discussed earlier in the chapter, as well as bureaucratic infrastructure that can be removed. Cycle reductions to 25 percent from "before" are not uncommon.

Pardon me for using that old *insight* word again. But the good CEO must develop or find someone with the *process insight* to analyze and better benchmark high risk or emerging problem areas in the process itself. Here is where so many tales are being told and books written that address common business processes in terms of quality or other terms to describe the opportunity and need.

> **Many times, businesses develop highly convoluted flows and paper trails and compartmentalized operations that not only inhibit the achievement of the goal, but obscure the goal entirely.**

Do you understand the process needed to launch a new product or service? How to reposition an existing product to extend its life? How to find a strategic partner to help grow the business? The insight and training necessary to understand and manage these processes are vital to the health of the business and to avoiding process bankruptcy. Though experience in the real world is beginning to show that you are generally not likely to totally remake a company using the fad-of-the-day tools offered in business books, the insights gained from undertaking the process and learning from campaign veterans (those people who are experienced in getting new products and services off the ground) are worth their weight in any precious metal.

A development schedule that calls for the finished product long after the customer wants it or the competitors release it is a sure sign of the need for an overhaul of the process of development.

Superior companies find extraordinarily fast ways to market with quality products. With today's narrow product windows, slow to market often means missing the window entirely.

> **Superior companies find extraordinarily fast ways to market with quality products. With today's narrow product windows, slow to market often means missing the window entirely.**

6

Defining the Context in Which We Work: A Pilot's Bag of Tools to Forecast and Navigate the Winds of Change

"Even a sailor at sea, when confronted with a thick fog, a blinding snowstorm, or a gale, can reduce speed or drop anchor and await more favorable conditions." – Malcolm Cagle

"According to the theory of aerodynamics, as may be readily demonstrated through wind tunnel experiments, the bumblebee is unable to fly. This is because the size, weight, and shape of his body in relation to the total wingspread make flying impossible. But the bumblebee, being ignorant of these scientific truths, goes ahead and flies anyway—and makes a little honey every day." – Sign found on a Fortune 50 manufacturing plant wall

May I first admit that I have been guilty more than once of enthusiastically developing products for a market that would not develop for years into the future? In some of these instances, the publicity value was probably worth the losses incurred. In others, there is no excuse. Enthusiasm for application of available technologies alone does not excuse bringing products to market that are not yet appropriate for the marketplace or cost-effective enough to justify their use.

You might say I was guilty of failing to understand the *context* for the product in that market.

> Enthusiasm for application of available technologies alone does not excuse bringing products to market that are not yet appropriate for the marketplace or cost-effective enough to justify their use.

Take for instance the early development of yield management systems for the hotel industry. Using the model then recently created by the airline industry with considerable success, I directed and participated in taking my company through development, marketing, and deployment of yield management systems for hotels. Not just any yield management systems, but systems built upon artificial intelligence platforms, using a programming language, LISP, unique to artificial intelligence applications.

The year was 1987. And you can bet the industry's curiosity was at its peak when the announcement of such a revolutionary system for predicting best rates and enhancing hotel revenues was first announced. At the annual trade show that year in Nashville, the room was set for 300 and quickly filled, leaving an equal number of conference attendees outside the door, unable to see the miracle system. A second session was quickly called, and it too filled with interested potential buyers.

We deployed the system in a beta environment at a well-known Boston hotel, whose senior manager demonstrated his skepticism by challenging the machine to a form of duel. He challenged the technology much as Paul Bunyan and his blue ox Babe were challenged to a duel of old versus new technology. After a week of actual use changing rates and making decisions about availability, the hotel manager asked if we were willing to turn the machine off and let him make the same type of decisions using no tools other than his intuition. We challenged him to the duel and did turn off the system for a week.

We knew we were in trouble when, at the end of the week, we turned the system on and it immediately made many, many thousands of dollars worth of revenue-enhancing decisions for past events, no longer controllable, but great proof of the effectiveness of the system. And the manager claimed victory anyway, even though no record was kept or metrics used to measure any of his efforts. Claiming victory, he directed that the advanced, artificial intelligence system be removed—to the dismay of all those within his property who had participated in the tests and proved the results.

So we made the decision to withdraw the product from the market after having sold only two at $150,000 each, knowing the market was not ready for our technology even if anxious to embrace its results.

The story has a great ending. We retreated to develop a software-only platform that addressed perhaps 80 percent of the opportunity, integrated well with the existing systems, presented itself only as a feature rather than a system, and was priced at a small fraction of the original complex but highly efficient tool. And we sold many of these simpler, cheaper "features."

In retrospect, we created and offered too much technology, too early to market, too complex for the user to grasp, requiring too much evangelizing and too many changes in customer operating procedure to put in place. All are signs of a company ignoring the context into which its product fits in the marketplace.

Perhaps you, too, have been guilty of failing to understand the context of failed market timing for a product that did not fit or arrived too soon to a market before proper platforms or tools were available at the right price. If so, you should have learned as I did that there is great value in understanding your customer. Focus groups, market studies, and simple prototype demos to existing and prospective customers all help position a product before larger expenditures of time and money are made into a doomed or premature product.

It is all about context. So let's digress for a moment and have a little fun exercising your mental abilities, and make a point about context management in the process. This one takes some concentration, so clear the decks.

Do You Need to Be a Weather Forecaster to Go Flying?

Here's a pop quiz. Think carefully before answering the two questions, even though neither is a trick question:

In general, winds flow around the Earth from west to east as a result of the spinning of the planet and of friction between the surface and the lower atmosphere. These winds increase with an increase in altitude, since the friction is less further from the surface. We call these the "prevailing westerlies," since they most always flow *from* the west. (For the sake of this exam, we'll not consider any of the other forces that could and do affect these winds.)

Question one: *Given the choice, would you rather fly toward due east or toward due west, considering the direction of the prevailing winds?*

Of course, the answer to the first question is "toward due east," making use of the tail wind *from the west*, behind you.

That question was to give you confidence and prepare you for the big one. Before you bail out on this more difficult second question, let's state up front that its point is to emphasize the importance of understanding time and context considerations in a complex world.

Now, assume you are in a small airplane that can travel at exactly 100 miles per hour. The winds today are *from the west* at fifty miles per hour. You will travel exactly 100 miles today, and the outbound leg of your trip takes you *from the west* heading due east with a tailwind of fifty miles per hour, while your return leg reverses course *heading due west* into the wind, which is still at fifty miles per hour.

Question two: *How long will it take to fly the combined outbound and return 200-mile course today?*

Well, now. You never expected to have to work out word problems in a book about efficient business processes, did you? But there's a good reason, as always.

We could merely have asked: "Will the headwind cancel the effects of the tailwind?" If so, you probably would have opted for the simple answer, as most people do. "Yes. A hundred miles to travel, times two legs of the trip at 100 miles per hour, would take two hours to fly." And this answer would have been correct if there were no winds.

Defining the Context in Which We Work

But you're smarter now, having worked out the problem. You discovered that, because of the fifty-mile-per-hour tailwind, your first leg takes only forty minutes. (That's 100 miles divided by [100 mph + 50 mph] = .66 hours or 40 minutes.) However, you calculated that your return leg, flying the identical course backwards, takes *two hours*! (That's 100 miles divided by [100 mph − 50 mph] = 2 hours.) The total flight lasts two hours and forty minutes, which is forty minutes longer than a flight with no wind at all.

So did we learn anything we can apply to extending our runway here? Sure. It takes more energy to fight the forces of nature or the trends in the marketplace (fly into the headwind) than to "go with the flow" (ride a tailwind), *because we are affected by the headwind for a longer period of time.*

Even the prevailing winds can be your enemy if you spend half your effort taking advantage and half your effort fighting them.

> **Even the prevailing winds can be your enemy if you spend half your effort taking advantage and half your effort fighting them.**

Now, if you'll indulge me for a few pages, let's make the problem of marketplace trends, or prevailing winds, more complex, reflecting the realities as they exist, and get a great mini-education about the weather as well. After all, every good pilot must understand the weather, just as every good C-level executive must understand the context in which s/he operates.

The great thing about the science of weather forecasting is that it is so unpredictable. All weather is caused by a transfer of heat between the Earth and the atmosphere, as warm air rises primarily from the equator as the equator is heated by the Sun. Air cools as it rises from the equator and disperses naturally both north and south as new air continues to rise from the equator. This air then falls back toward Earth, having traveled both north and south to about thirty degrees north and south latitudes respectively in a very predictable pattern.

As this sea of air sinks, it dries and it again picks up heat, warmed by the Earth itself. It is this warm, dry air that is primarily responsible for our Earth's vast dry deserts that span across the globe, mostly centered about these thirty-degree north and south latitudes where the hot, dry air returns to Earth. If there were no other forces of nature, there would be only hot, moist air rising from the equator and hot, dry deserts equally spaced between cooler, wet regions on the globe.

But the science of weather is not that simple, nor is the science of predicting the flow of market demand.

Why is this a science that is more unpredictable, much like market forces? Friction from the Earth's surface *slows the prevailing westerly winds* as the Earth rotates, bending the wind's path up to forty-five degrees as the dropping air returns to the surface. The speed of the rotating Earth is near 1,000 miles per hour at the equator, but exactly zero at the poles. So air travels at slower speeds further north.

Add more complexity, just as in the market. Add water. As the Sun heats the waters of the Earth's oceans, evaporation pulls moisture into the atmosphere. Large masses of air form over the oceans, picking up more moisture from the water, moving in irregular paths as the air masses advance toward land *driven by the prevailing winds*, but frustrated by areas of high pressure often formed over the warm, dry deserts.

Add changes in temperature. Each morning on the Earth's land masses, as the Sun heats the surface, these air masses warm and rise. As the air rises, it cools and can absorb less moisture than when warm. The moisture separates from the air around it and becomes visible in the form of clouds.

Remaining with the science of weather for just a moment longer, weather forecasters know the basic truth that the more heat and moisture present, the more unstable air becomes. Afternoons in many parts of the globe are times for recurring thunderstorms caused by the unstable air masses as they rise from the Earth and are *pushed by the prevailing winds*, forcing the air masses across mountains or gently rising terrain in vast open areas such as in the deserts of the southwestern United States. Additional storms form as a result of unstable moist air masses flowing from warm oceans, such as in

Defining the Context in Which We Work 107

the South Atlantic and Gulf of Mexico. These sometimes grow to hurricane size. These storms can rise as high as the stratosphere, 60,000 feet above the Earth at the equator.

Think of the immensity of these forces: wind, heat, water. Equate them to the prevailing forces in the marketplace: monetary policy, governmental regulation, sector demand, competition.

A pilot who deliberately takes off on a flight without knowing the existing and forecasted weather along his or her route is taking a chance far greater than necessary. Even the largest aircraft that flies above the Earth, the 747, is not immune to the effects of the weather. All commercial air carriers require that their pilots chart courses that avoid known thunderstorm activity by at least ten miles. The strength of the storms often exceed the force of a nuclear bomb, and pilots have learned the hard way to respect nature's force by remaining a respectable distance from such storms.

Like the marketplace, weather can change in an instant. A clear morning can turn into zero visibility in fog within a few minutes, as the Earth is heated by the rising Sun to the exact temperature at which the air can no longer absorb its moisture. Thunderstorms can form in minutes, grow to unbelievable heights, and burn themselves out, all within less than an hour.

So the prevailing winds are frustrated by heat and moisture. Unpredictable changes give rise to unexpected bad weather and unexpected hot, sunny days in the middle of winter.

And in the marketplace, product trends can be frustrated by innovation, price competition, and the fickle nature of fads. There is a science to forecasting the market, but the constant and changing research necessary is not easily available to most early-stage companies. But the signs of such marketplace changes certainly are available, even if they come from employees in the field, early adapter customer requests, and consultants who also deal with the larger companies.

The trick is to use the fewest resources possible to discern these forces that frustrate the prevailing market direction, finding niches for products and services that open and close but are often either too small or too quick to appear for the larger market leaders to address.

So the weather and the marketplace have much in common. Both give signs of predictability if the observer understands the science behind the changes observed. Both offer prevailing winds or trends with which pilots and companies must recon in order to conserve and extend resources—money and fuel. Both are fickle and frustrating by their nature, with numerous forces that change the flow and require constant awareness and response.

> **The trick is to use the fewest resources possible to discern these forces that frustrate the prevailing market direction, finding niches for products and services that open and close but are often either too small or too quick to appear for the larger market leaders to address.**

Weather forecasting was one of the first major applications addressed by the early computer industry using the largest mainframes because of the computing power necessary to develop models to predict the flows of the winds. We have since become quite proficient at forecasting the weather, using satellites that photograph the areas of moisture and their tracks across the globe. Pilots now obtain a thorough weather briefing through their desktop or notebook computers, and are expected to launch their craft only if and when they have satisfied themselves that weather will not interfere with the safety of their flight. The responsibility for the decision to fly or wait out the weather rests solely upon the pilot of the craft, not upon the weatherman or any other individual on the ground.

Yet up to half of the accidents each year involving aircraft are weather-related, and up to 80 percent of these are ultimately considered to be *pilot error*. "The pilot flew into adverse weather conditions beyond his or his craft's ability to control," reads the accident report time and again.

What is the lesson we can gleam from all this?

- Pilots have sophisticated resources to forecast the weather but still manage to make fatal mistakes on a regular basis.
- There is very little available science in forecasting the business environment, so we are at a disadvantage even as we start our journey.
- The unpredictability of the future, especially in technology-driven industries, is made even more so by the rapid obsolescence of hardware as newer, faster chips and processors come to market, enabling new opportunities for breakthroughs on a regular basis.

But there is the opportunity. We know that, over time, the winds prevail from the west and that, at times, there are periods of unusual weather—some bad, some good—brought about by forces that frustrate the prevailing winds. If we could only take advantage of the prevailing winds, avoid the rough weather when it arrives, and bask in the good weather for a disproportionate time, we would greatly increase our odds of long-term success (or survival).

So what does this have to do with our business decisions and extending the runway?

> **If we could only take advantage of the prevailing winds, avoid the rough weather when it arrives, and bask in the good weather for a disproportionate time, we would greatly increase our odds of long-term success (or survival).**

Translating all this into lessons for our businesses, we plan to make use of tools to gain insight, spotting the prevailing trends in our industry, and then forecast the near-term changes so we might plan our business opportunities to coincide with the good weather, avoiding the bad weather as much as possible.

Of course, we should try our best to steer our business into a tailwind whenever possible and use less energy moving toward our goal.

- Don't be too early to enter a market that does not understand the context of the product or the usefulness of the product itself. The effort defies the benefit gained by first-movers paying the price of paving the way with expenditure of time and money to seed a new market.
- Plan for extra time and cost to adhere to standards, regulations, position against competitors, and to educate the market.
- Take advantage of the excitement generated by the press, industry buzz, and new technology breakthroughs that create standard platforms upon which to host your product or service.

Others may fly directly against the prevailing winds and reach their goal. But the longer the journey, the more likely they are to run out of fuel going in their direction than you are in yours.

So we learn to manage within the context of our environment, to move with the prevailing winds and use less energy or resources to achieve the goal.

Context Management

"Help Me! I'm Lost Up Here!"—Context Bankruptcy

Can you put up with yet another aviation story? It is a true story, which I witnessed years ago when stationed at the Memphis Naval Air Station while in the service. (By the way, I am not the student pilot in this story.)

The student pilot took off from Memphis on his first long cross-country solo flight, having been signed off by his flight instructor as prepared for the adventure. The student had carefully planned his flight using the proper charts and had transferred the distances he had measured between checkpoints to a flight log form, which he then used to calculate time en route to each checkpoint and fuel required for the flight. The exercise is known as *pilotage* using the map, compass, and clock to make sure your flight is tracking the desired path and that you are traveling at the expected ground speed—therefore using the expected amount of fuel. Note that pilotage is still taught, even with the advent of moving maps and global positioning systems in most every cockpit as a backup in the case of equipment failure or power loss. In this case, there was no GPS system aboard, and this student, in his panic, was unable to make sense of and use his radio navigation aids.

Forty minutes into the flight, with three hours of fuel aboard, the pilot began to sweat profusely. He was lost. He had been following the flight with his finger on his map, cross-checking checkpoints on the map against those he saw outside his window, but had missed seeing the large water tower near the diagonally crossing railroad tracks he had expected to see ten minutes ago.

Student pilots learn to fly first using the map and compass, then later using more sophisticated radio and global positioning navigation. Although our student had basic radio navigation knowledge, his panic was real. The Tennessee countryside all looked the same to him. There were no immediately discernible landmarks within his line of sight. What could he do to solve his predicament? He could continue on the same course until seeing any recognizable landmark; he could radio any of several resources for help; or he could merely turn in a direction that might cross a major highway or railroad track, allowing him to then follow the track to a known landmark.

Here's a common parallel for the business world. Our hapless student chose *none of the above*. Instead, he turned first in one direction, then another, desperately searching for some landmark he could recognize on his map. After ten minutes of this, he was so lost he was completely unaware of his probable location. He had completely lost situational awareness. Remember that he began with three logical options, all previously covered in ground school training and his instructor's pre-briefing. And he chose none of the above.

There is business lesson here. Choosing to do nothing in the face of obvious signs of difficulty is an option, but perhaps the least likely option for success. There are always clues to guide you, some from your past experience, some from past formal education or training. Resources are always available to help make the decision if you know where to find them.

> **Choosing to do nothing in the face of obvious signs of difficulty is an option, but perhaps the least likely option for success. There are always clues to guide you, some from your past experience, some from past formal education or training. Resources are always available to help make the decision if you know where to find them.**

What happened to our student who chose to do nothing? He ultimately made an unscheduled landing in a plowed field, landing against the plowed lines, and flipped his small craft needlessly on its back as it hit the first plowed furl. Unhurt except for a bruised ego, the pilot learned much more than he bargained for that day at the expense of relatively minor repairs to the rented aircraft. Upon returning to his home airfield, his instructor controlled his voice carefully, covering again the logic of the planned backups, all of which the student had ignored.

There was a fourth option, allowed his instructor. And this is the lesson we all need to remember in the context of thinking out a problem with a clear mind and using any helpful resources available. The instructor reminded the hapless pilot that the Mississippi River runs right down the left corner of Tennessee from north to south, passing Memphis in the process. Knowing he never crossed that giant river during his flight, the pilot could have merely turned northwest, maintained that course until seeing the big, muddy river, and turned south until finding Memphis. The solution was really that easy, buried within the false complexity of the student's panic and myopic vision that often accompanies such attacks.

Often, business leaders act the same way as this pilot. The shame is that most believe they know enough to complete the flight, even if they start out with no map or plan at all.

Defining the Context in Which We Work

Our plan composed of the goal, strategies, and tactics to move us toward the goal is our map and flight log. It is, however, merely an exercise for us to prepare such a plan *if it will be ignored or if it contains no method of measuring the checkpoints along the course.*

But even more tragic is the entrepreneur-pilot who takes off without a map or plan at all, perhaps because he has lived in the area for years and certainly knows the territory.

There are three very important things to consider before betting the success of your flight upon certain knowledge of the terrain. First, the terrain looks entirely different from altitude than it does from the ground., just as the business environment never seems to match that which we studied in college or B-school or experienced in a previous enterprise. Second, the terrain changes over time as development reshapes the landscape as you knew it before. Time itself molds changes that should be expected. And third, visibility changes drastically with changes in the weather. The world looks very different on a hazy day than when the ceiling and visibility are unlimited. Marketplace demand suffers from storms and eddies based upon external forces such as raw material supply, geopolitical events and stock market mood swings.

Launching a product or business in any fast-moving industry requires that the person responsible for the launch understand the marketplace (*the terrain*), the competition (*changes to the terrain due to development*), the niches that may contain an urgent demand for the product, the maturity of the market, and the appropriate channels of distribution. Further, all of these factors may be influenced by the current state of the economy itself (*visibility due to weather*).

And finally, many businesses will be affected by the regulatory environment of their industry. For example, accounting software unable to cope with value-added taxation rules would not be usable in Canada or Europe; health care provider billing software must conform to the rules of the Health Insurance Portability and Accountability Act and Medicare billing to be usable, no matter how elegant the solution offered.

Entering the market with anything less than this knowledge and a plan with a backup is tantamount to taking off without a map. Events that influence your product sales success may not be understood in the context of the real-world environment in which they take place. So reactions to the events may be inappropriate and damaging to the success of the product or company, just as the pilot's reaction to being lost was out of context with the obvious terrain information available—and completely out of place, considering his careful plan and earlier briefing.

> **Entering the market with anything less than this knowledge and a plan with a backup is tantamount to taking off without a map.**

Yet it happens every day. We only hear of the results when a company runs out of runway and the result is documented in the papers, court records, or industry gossip. But in fact, the results are almost certainly predictable the moment the pilot selects *none of the above* and in doing so fails to at least call for help.

So this is *context bankruptcy*. The opportunity to navigate safely depends upon having a plan, knowing alternatives, and calling for help at the appropriate time if it becomes necessary. The next step, after ignoring these, is the first step toward context bankruptcy. Barring pure luck—finding a landing field in front of you in the midst of a vast plain—the unscheduled termination of the venture is certain.

Plan the flight; then fly the plan.

Use current charts and data. Learn all you can about the weather (marketplace climate) as it is right now and is forecast for your planned time en route.

Only then, take off. It's as simple as that.

> ***Plan the flight; then fly the plan.***

So now we've looked at all five forms of resource bankruptcy that can bring fragile (and even solid) businesses down. All of these are controllable by the founders, board, stakeholders, or managers at some stage of development and growth of a company.

Context Insight!

Never Becoming Lost While Looking at the Map: Sidestepping Context Bankruptcy

"Help me! I'm lost up here." These are the words we used to begin our story about the Memphis student pilot without a clue as to his position, because he hadn't a clue as to the context in which he found himself—the big picture that placed Memphis on the Mississippi River and always west of his position.

In business, we are all subjected to the same challenges—understanding the context within which we work - the big picture. How far along is the competition with its competitive product? How does the competition price its product? Is the industry near the end of its current growth cycle? Or are we at the headwaters of a stream that leads to the mother of all rivers? Has this become primarily a *cash cow* opportunity? Is the regulatory environment changing and forcing new decisions to accommodate those changes?

Insight into the context within which we work is like using satellite photos to know today's weather and getting a good grasp upon tomorrow's forecast. No pilot would launch into a hurricane or a line of thunderstorms. And no one would fly toward such a cataclysmic ocean of air intentionally if he or she had received a weather briefing based upon an up-to-date forecast.

But weather forecasts contain common warnings that, if always followed to the letter, would cause the pilot to cancel every flight for months at a time. During summertime, forecasts for many areas of the country contain the phrase "occasional afternoon thunderstorms." And during the winter, there is, "Chance of icing in clouds above (six, seven, eight) thousand feet."

So how does a pilot deal with balancing risk against the time-saving benefits of completion of the flight? How does a pilot put those common daily warnings in context and make maximum safe utilization of his or her aircraft by canceling just a few percent of intended flights over time because of inclement weather? Experienced pilots develop an insight into the limits that both the pilot and aircraft can push safely, and plan flights with alternatives based upon prudent decision points. They use tools such as thunderstorm detection instruments, on-board weather radar and reports from other pilots flying the same route.

The less-experienced visual pilot's best weapon to combat these common forecasted possibilities is the 180-degree turn to reverse course and find safety.

How about us? Will we become so conservative that our competition's moves will force us to forgo development of a project, lower prices without a clear picture of relative product strengths, or even abandon a niche market entirely because the big players are hyperactive?

Having earned or learned context insight into the probable results of our actions will help us spot and evaluate the early signs of trouble that allow us to launch our project or product, even if the forecast contains the usual cautions we've heard so many times before. Or are we skilled enough that our well-developed context insights open other alternatives than retreat?

Once again, the similarity to flying is uncanny. With proper context insight, we can develop alternative plans in case we experience violent storms that seriously threaten our capacity to continue on course. And we should use every resource we can muster to find ways to understand the context of our position so we might safely continue rather than retreat.

How about yourself? Have you become so embroiled in the day-to-day management of your business that you have lost some or most of the context sensitivity you had when you started? Do you have an uncanny knowledge of your competitor's position and the market's condition? Have you been out with your customers and prospects enough to know the coming challenges to your company and your product?

Today, as a result of changes in demand, the context of your products' uses to solve problems that may have changed since the time of original development, and other external forces, the target market for your company's products may be changing rapidly. Working from old data or failing to obtain direct, continuous, frequent feedback from customers is a recipe for eventual failure, as the target market moves away from your center of focus.

> **Working from old data or failing to obtain direct, continuous, frequent feedback from customers is a recipe for eventual failure, as the target market moves away from your center of focus.**

If your context sensitivity, or insight, is low and getting worse, it may be the right time to seek assistance. You can look for experts who are experienced in tracking current customer needs on an ongoing basis to advise you, or you can take the opportunity to recreate your executive organization to place emphasis upon the need to both tend to the day-to-day business and look outward toward new opportunities at the same time. That is why the founder of a business or a venture capitalist investing in a company often looks to hire a professional manager at a critical point in the company's growth, often allowing the founder to return to his or her strongest areas—product design or marketing—as part of the transition.

All companies undergo a predictable series of reorganizations or crises that come in cycles during their growth stages. Often, these are brought about by the late recognition that the context has shifted while the company has not. Depending upon the type of operation, these cycles can come every $3 to $6 million in revenue growth (*the every $3 million crisis*) for the first three or four of these cycles, and less often thereafter. It is at each of these critical crisis points that the board and founder-entrepreneur should reassess whether they and their team are in the correct positions to provide superior growth management, or if the time has come for a transition of one or more of the senior team, including the CEO, into a new role.

Having the right CEO at the helm for the appropriate stage of a company's growth is probably the most critical success factor in the evolution of a business. There is little place for a founder's ego in making such a decision to transition management because of the immense cost of a mistake. In the real world, however, the CEO slot is often filled by the founder(s) for years longer than it should be, to the detriment of the organization's full potential. On the positive side, many founder CEOs can and do transition through all the phases of growth and crisis.

And while we are discussing the CEO's strengths, we should look to examine the management team at each of these easily identifiable crisis points in a company's growth. The entrepreneur often finds himself or herself with a management team not by design but by happenstance. Those who helped bring the idea to its first stages of reality are often made managers in critical areas of the business. When this happens, as the business grows and management roles change with maturity, it becomes increasingly difficult to make objective decisions to shuffle or replace the pioneer senior managers, even if for the good of the business.

An objective view of the goal and the management resources positioned to reach that goal is absolutely necessary. The same rules apply to the management team as to the CEO regarding the cyclical crisis review points. Often, the crisis is brought on by one or more members of the senior team reaching his or her level of incompetence and thereby blocking others from continuing to grow the company.

> **All companies undergo a predictable series of reorganizations or crises that come in cycles during their growth stages. Often, these are brought about by the late recognition that the context has shifted while the company has not.**

Developing insight means, among other things, developing context sensitivity. When the company shifts or the environment shifts away from the company, you should be able to spot the movement early enough to take alternative action, resetting the course toward your goal.

Your team extends well beyond your management and even your employees. The effective teams usually include either of two types of boards to advise or direct management, adding missing areas of experience, insight, and expertise to the company in the process.

The company may form an advisory board to help guide management in specific areas of technical, marketing, or industry strategy. Advisory boards are generally informal, members are invited at the pleasure of the CEO, and an offer to pay a reasonable board fee in options or cash is appropriate, depending upon the size of the company and the relationship between the CEO and members of the board. Since the advice of this board is only that, there is less risk in selecting members of an advisory board than a formal board of directors. However, following bad advice from any person or group can still prove very expensive.

Companies of any size, those seeking to go public, and those funded by outside capital resources other than an angel (i.e., family member or friend) generally must form formal boards of directors to represent the shareholders and oversee the operations of the company and its CEO. Although some financial institutions will require that their investments be protected by the granting of one or more board seats, in most cases the board is still generally recruited and named by the founders of the business. This has rapidly changed as best practices dictate that nominating committees of boards do not include insiders, especially the CEO.

Venture investors almost always insist upon board seats and, as outsiders, often fill the role of both the audit and compensation committees, the two required committees on any board.

The opportunity for the board to make significant, strategic impact is greatest when the founders recruit board members to fill remaining seats for their business expertise, perspective, and contacts, not as a reward for friendship *or passive investment*. Outside board members should be paid for their services in stock options or cash rather than on a per-meeting basis. Inside board members or those representing investors are usually not paid separately for their board work. As a resource, the board is critical to the success of the company if the founders elect only those with a contribution to make and then review all strategic and major financial matters of the company with the board. In a company where the CEO is not the majority shareholder, the board serves a much more critical role; it is this organization that must represent the shareholders' interests and assure the protection of their investment by asking tough questions and then retaining or changing the CEO based upon the CEO's performance and responses to challenges.

> **The opportunity for the board to make significant, strategic impact is greatest when the founders recruit board members to fill remaining seats for their business expertise, perspective, and contacts, not as a reward for friendship *or passive investment.***

So to avoid the terrible consequences of context bankruptcy, take positive actions such as those shared above. Review your own, your management's, and your board's strengths and move decisively to add strength where needed. Perhaps a more horrible thought than picturing yourself completely lost without a clue to your position is the thought that you could be in such shape with no idea that you're even lost.

7

Interrelationships: Optimal Management of Competing Demands

"The winds and waves are always on the side of the ablest navigators." – Gibbon

"If you come to a fork in the road, take it." – Yogi Berra

Your Skills in Complex Management

Professional pilots are predictable in many ways. They train in full-motion simulators on the average of six hours every six months, practicing crew coordination, emergency recovery techniques that could not safely be practiced in an aircraft, and most of all, the conditioned responses to challenges they may never face in their working lifetimes—but that, as a result of their training, they would recognize and respond to at the first sign of a developing problem.

Pilots, as a community, train in these realistic simulations so they may react to crises with calm, efficient responses appropriate to the event or combination of events that may challenge them.

Externally Induced Crises

July 19, 1989. The captain and two cockpit crew members of a United DC-10 were making routine preparations for descent into Chicago O'Hare when the captain felt a sudden pull on the yoke and shudder of the plane. Engine number three, located in the tail of the craft, ceased to produce power. That they could see from their gauges. But the pilots had no way then of knowing that the plane's tail engine had exploded, severing the hydraulic lines that controlled both the elevators (vertical motion) and the rudder (turns). Later, it was found that a crack in the engine's fan assembly had been the cause.

Nothing they had ever practiced in their many simulator sessions came close to what they were experiencing. No DC-10 had ever experienced such an incident before, and the manufacturer's operations manuals did not contain anything that would help the captain with the decisions he would make and the actions he would try over the next hour.

But the plane continued to fly straight and level. It was unresponsive to attempts to turn or descend. The captain declared an emergency, communicating his problem with the air traffic control center. On United's company frequency, he attempted to find expert help from anyone who might contribute with a solution to the problem of controlling the aircraft.

The captain and his two crew members kept a cool head, discussed their alternatives as a team, and began to experiment carefully using differential power from the two wing-mounted engines to control the aircraft, reducing power slowly to descend and reducing power to one engine to turn in that direction.

Knowing the immense risk they were taking, but without a viable alternative, the crew elected to accept the recommendation from the control center that the flight divert to Sioux City, Iowa, nearer their present position than Chicago, and a less-populated area. For more than an hour, the crew nursed the craft first north and then, after several uncontrollable turns, south for final approach. Maintaining control under almost impossible odds in an environment they had never been prepared for, the crew kept control right down to within feet of the runway, before the aircraft veered left at touchdown.

Of the 296 aboard, 184 survived that accident, all because of the cool control and teamwork approach of the captain, cockpit crew, and a special resource team at United's facility in San Francisco.

Interrelationships 123

The three used resources available to them by radio and their own ingenuity to solve problems as a team. Their almost unbelievable feat was rewarded by their actions saving the lives of most of the passengers and crew onboard. The aviation community hailed the captain and crew for their show of uncommon skill under immense pressure.

What went right here? External events overwhelmed the crew, who were forced to improvise without a precedent to guide them. In any situation, pilots are taught first and foremost to *fly the plane*, to make secondary all other considerations, even including radioing for help. More accidents occur from loss of control of the aircraft than all other direct causes of accidents combined. Distractions of any kind reduce the focus and increase the risk of loss of control.

The pilots worked together as a team, with the captain drawing the best from his crew (inside and outside of the plane) right to touchdown. There was no last-minute shift of responsibilities, no lack of communication in the cockpit, and no question as to the goal to be achieved. They sought expert help from the best sources available, using radio communication as their window to the outside to extend the resources of the combined internal and external crew.

And most importantly, they continued to maintain control of the ship.

> **Distractions of any kind reduce the focus and increase the risk of loss of control.**

Externally induced crises can affect businesses with the same potential for devastation. From forces of nature such as tornados, hurricanes, fires, or floods, to manmade forces such as criminal acts by or toward your employees, to deliberate salvos at the company such as discrimination lawsuits, you may someday be challenged in ways you can hardly imagine today.

So how would you react to a crisis brought about by external forces beyond your control? Would you seek help while boldly rallying your crew and still maintaining control over the ship? Pilots train all their professional lives toward that remote possibility, but no one is suggesting that the same rigorous training program be created for business executives.

However, somewhere nearby, there is someone who has been in almost exactly the same situation as you may someday find yourself when thrust into the center of an emergency induced by outside events. Knowing the availability of resources and where to find them should be, in light of this example, a priority not to be ignored for another day. And having a crisis plan that has been developed by your company to cover at least the first steps in crisis response coordination would go a very long way toward focusing the crew during the most critical first hours or days following an externally induced crisis.

> **Having a crisis plan that has been developed by your company to cover at least the first steps in crisis response coordination would go a very long way toward focusing the crew during the most critical first hours or days following an externally induced crisis.**

Pilot Error: The Self-Induced Crisis

January 25, 1990. After a five-hour flight from Medillin, Columbia, a Brazilian Avianca Airlines 707 approached New York Center airspace from the south for landing at JFK Airport. It was the height of the evening rush, when aircraft from all over the United States funnel into this airspace, feeding passengers into a complex network of connecting flights, both domestic and international. Visibility was poor due to low clouds and rain. Visual approaches could not be used. They would have increased efficiency by permitting reduced separation between landing aircraft.

The pilot and his two crew members knew their fuel state was at the edge of the legal limit with slightly under an hour and a half in reserve following their long flight north. Instructed to hold for a delayed approach, the crew acknowledged the instruction by New York Center's controller handling the sector of the airspace containing their craft. For over an hour, the crew flew the required race track pattern with two-minute legs, all without transmitting their ever-critical fuel state to the controller. During that time and including the hour before, thirty-three other flight crews elected to divert to their alternate destinations because of the long holds at JFK. Finally, the craft was cleared for the approach and began the process of following the path to lower altitude and proper alignment for landing at JFK.

Perhaps due to the high winds and low ceilings, the crew missed the approach the first time and notified the controller that a go-around was being commenced. There was less than twenty minutes of fuel on board at best, and the crew informed the controller that the craft did not have enough fuel to divert to Boston, the designated alternate. Significantly, the crew did not make their very low fuel state clear to the controller, nor did they declare an emergency. They began to climb again into the holding pattern and waited for re-sequencing for landing.

Perhaps the captain felt he would be lucky, and would be given clearance to land with plenty of time (ten minutes of fuel left by then). Or perhaps he thought his understated confession that he was low on fuel would result in the controller's taking the initiative and expediting their arrival. As the crew climbed again to restart their approach procedure, they discussed among themselves the ever-increasingly critical situation. But neither the pilot nor the co-pilot made any effort to declare the emergency that would have cleared them immediately for a direct course to the airport and an expedited approach.

And as the crew turned over Long Island, a full eighty-nine minutes of delay later, and as they made the first of several turns to align their craft for final approach, they acknowledged among themselves that the gauges showed no remaining fuel, "that they must be flying on fumes alone." The cockpit voice recorder recorded those words right before the four engines flamed out one immediately after another from fuel starvation, as the grand old 707 became a large, inefficient glider, crashing a few minutes later in landing configuration, without a drop of fuel aboard, in a wooded section of Long Island.

Seventy-three died needlessly in that accident. The cause was clearly pilot error—failure to take control of a situation that was at first routine and then a full-blown emergency brought about by the crew's *indecision*.

So what kind of pilot would you have been in this situation? Would you have confessed your plight to someone who could help but would perhaps chastise you for allowing yourself to get into the situation? Would you be intimidated when finding yourself in a foreign element, as this crew might have been, finding themselves in a foreign country and in one of the busiest air corridors on Earth?

How would you exercise your leadership in a crisis that begins as benignly as the frog's predicament when finding himself in that kettle of warm water, heating up slowly, almost imperceptibly up to the boiling point?

We could use airline analogies all day to illustrate traits of leadership and responses to crisis…

…The communications misunderstanding between crew and ground control that led to the takeoff crash of two 747s on Tenerife, Canary Islands, in 1977 that killed 582—the worst disaster in aviation history…

…The misreading of an engine power gauge by two inexperienced Air Florida pilots in a Washington, D.C., National Airport takeoff that caused them to use less than maximum available power on takeoff in a mistaken attempt to prevent engine damage that would not have occurred with the application of full power, leaving the aircraft with too little power to climb, and directly causing the crash of their aircraft into the Potomac River…

…The pilots of the Southwest 737 who decided, against training and their airline's manuals, to add what turned out to be forty-four knots of extra speed on a steep and bumpy final approach into Burbank on March 5, 2000, "for the wife and kids"—a move made in the name of safety that resulted instead in the plane landing long, overrunning the runway, and stopping in a gas station across the street. Or Southwest flight 1248, another 737 inbound to Chicago Midway on December 8, 2005, whose pilots also landed long and using extra speed. Both planes were directed onto final by controllers who noted a tailwind, exactly the opposite of ideal landing conditions. Sometimes controllers in such situations, certainly expecting a safe end to the flight, jokingly instruct the pilots to "stop at the end (of the runway), speed and altitude permitting." Obviously.

...The spectacular flying skills of two 737 Aloha Airline pilots to a successful landing after the upper skin of their aircraft peeled off like a banana peel at 24,000 feet, following years of stressful pressurizations in a corrosive salt-water environment...

All of these incidents led to new rules, new procedures, and new pages in the operations manuals to guide controllers, maintenance crews, and flight crews to avoid similar incidents.

But it is precisely the stark contrast between the aviation and business environments that leads us to cite these examples of good and bad use of management skill and available resources to overcome adversity and solve seemingly insurmountable problems.

The message here is that resources are available, sometimes at a moment's notice, to guide you through challenges. Knowing when and how to use those resources is a challenge to the business "pilot" who must train in preparation for the crisis that hopefully will never come by networking among associates, always searching for resources to add to his or her list, and remaining alert to the early signs of impending crisis.

There is also a message that relates to the style you use as pilot in command to get the most out of your crew. That is, the more you share the responsibility between you and your cockpit crew, the more likely you are to receive critical feedback and useful contribution by the crew in managing the flight tasks.

> **The more you share the responsibility between you and your cockpit crew, the more likely you are to receive critical feedback and useful contribution by the crew...**

The co-pilot and flight engineer of the Avianca plane that ran out of fuel were major factors in the accident, because they did not assert themselves in front of the pilot when their input might still have changed the course of events. Was the pilot responsible for their acquiescence because of an autocratic nature? Were they just as intimidated by the environment as he? Would they have done better with prior training simulating the high-pressure environment of the New York airspace at rush hour?

"Crew Resource Management"—Mastering Crew Coordination

In many universities, business departments frequently offer seminars for senior company management based upon the management styles a CEO can use with his employees. These seminars often include a self-evaluation test to help the manager determine his individual style and therefore how he might interact with those around him most effectively.

We heartily recommend the day or two's time such a seminar takes, if you haven't been to one before.

Most airlines and Flight Safety International, a professional pilot training organization, provide courses to commercial pilots in *crew resource management*, a phrase developed to describe not only the skills required to most effectively work with fellow crew members (airborne and ground-based), but also the psychological elements that come into play in a superior-subordinate crew environment.

Businesspeople could gain much from these interactive sessions, because many of the problems uncovered and dealt with are the same. Take the "I won't make waves because this person controls my future" syndrome. Or "If I warn him of this problem, he'll only jump down my throat." And "Even though we may crash, if I take over the controls to save this ship, it's mutiny!" (Does this mean die together, preserving the integrity of the relationship?)

The first two examples above occur in businesses every day. You may be able to identify with either or both in a close, too-personal way—drawing from your past or present experience.

Interrelationships

As silly as the last one sounds, it has been found to be the root cause of several commercial aircraft accidents over the years, and it takes two forms. Either the captain says, "Shut up! I've got it!" or the co-pilot asks, "Are you okay?" all the way into the ground. The results are the same. The issue deals with pilot incapacitation while at the controls, whether mental or physical. To that extent, there is little similarity with the business environment. But there are instances in which the CEO of a business is away from the business for extended periods of time for medical emergency, vacation, or business travel that become very close pantomimes of the airline captain's refusal or inability to delegate even when obviously unable to control the ship for the time being.

So once a crew can be taught when and how to interact in a crisis without fear of reprimand, the course turns to exploring the true division of responsibilities between captain and crew and how to make the most efficient use of the human resources in and beyond the airline cabin. Since each captain has his or her own management style, the organization chart and written job description may not apply exactly the same way each time a new crew member joins the group, whether for a single flight or a full month's schedule.

And in this material way, companies run the same way as commercial aircraft cockpits. The insertion of a temporary or permanent change at the executive level will alter the interaction between all of the senior crew members. Until all are quite satisfied that the captain's actions match his or her words, the crew will not work together as a unit to the maximum efficiency level it could achieve.

> **The insertion of a temporary or permanent change at the executive level will alter the interaction between all of the senior crew members. Until all are quite satisfied that the captain's actions match his or her words, the crew will not work together as a unit to the maximum efficiency level it could achieve.**

About Your Personal Flying Skills...

Well, to carry this book's analogy to its logical conclusion: you have your aircraft. And certainly you have your pilot's license. After the time you've spent in ground school and flight training, you should be proud of your accomplishments.

True, without the extra work and time to earn your instrument ticket, you'll be limited to visual flight below the 18,000-feet lower boundary of Class A airspace reserved for the big boys. In the meantime, the rules prohibit you from flying inside clouds. That means you'll have to plan later-morning takeoffs on days when there is morning fog, and you'll have to skip a few flights on days when the overcast never clears, where the instrument ticket would have let you punch through the overcast and fly above the layer of clouds.

You know you could fly with a little more precision if you had a bit more training toward the instrument rating, but who's going to notice in the meantime? And weather knowledge? You've got enough to understand when not to fly.

But you are proud of your aircraft. It's state of the art. Retractable gear, powerful engine with variable pitch propeller, turbocharged for high-altitude flight. Full instrument flight rules instrumentation, too, including all the latest avionics, with a satellite global positioning receiver for direct navigation and an autopilot that can hold altitude as well as heading with precision.

Here we go again. Need I point out that what we have here is a mismatch between pilot and craft? Not only is the aircraft capable of flying higher than your license limit, but it is equipped to safely carry out missions under instrument conditions, which is more than we can say for the pilot.

What a shame. A pilot without the skills to use the aircraft to achieve its best performance is limiting the value of the aircraft to that of one the pilot *should be flying*. All the rest is comfort and bragging rights.

Interrelationships

If you're that pilot, get an instrument ticket now—or at least hire a certified instrument flight instructor to go along with you on trips so you can learn while utilizing your aircraft efficiently, unless you're only a hobbyist and aspire to nothing more than being a Sunday airplane driver.

The same is true for you and your business. We've warned about the five resource bankruptcies and explained insights to spot and combat them, all toward helping you gain insight into extending your runway.

You recognize that you are constantly learning – from customers who turn out to be excellent teachers, from competitors who make mistakes that are visible and perhaps obvious in hindsight, from industry resources that are willing to help you direct and grow your enterprise if only asked.

We near the end of our journey, having crossed many a time zone. One final stop…and of all places, it's a hanger. It's an aviation custom called "hanger flying," as old as flying itself. All of us old salts do it…telling stories of our successes and close calls, of our glory moments and about how "I learned about flying from that."

And everybody has a story. You've just got to dig deep enough to find it. One of the messages of this book is that entrepreneurs and managers need to build networks—resources to turn to when the problems or opportunities are beyond your experience—to do a little hangar flying as a way of sharing, learning, developing vision.

Aircraft hangers are often messy places. Chairs and old couches are strewn about almost haphazardly. But toward the end of the day, young students and old salts alike seem to migrate toward the comfort of their favorite place, ready to relax and enjoy stories of great flying feats from moments or years ago.

Now, don't get me wrong. Corporate and commercial hangers that house the really big iron are almost always spotless extensions of the office environment, with the offices of the chief pilot majestically positioned between a window overlooking the hanger and the executive offices of the flight department housed in the same spotless building. But even here, old salts can't resist the urge to pull a chair across the carpet and navigate once again those distant storms.

But this isn't one of those glass and gleaming corporate showplaces. Here we can just grab a seat on that old couch in the corner and spend a last minute reviewing what we've discussed and making an action plan.

Summing It All Up: Locking the Hanger for the Night

We've spent some time together, exploring some of the dark corners that are rarely discussed when speaking of business management. Resources—five classes of them—that provide both an opportunity to excel and a time trap into which we can fall. *Time, money, relationships, process, and context.* Understanding the best ways to leverage each is the key to success in your business career and for your enterprise.

And understanding the need to manage as a team—a crew—becomes as important as honing individual management skills. You recognize that the team reaches beyond the doors of the business and can include all forms of help.

You've agreed to think about context of your own vision, to test whether your plan flies with or against the prevailing winds. And finally, you've thought about your personal skills in the management of complex interrelationships of resource challenges—both internal and external to the organization.

Well, you can't stop here. Your next move might be to gather the senior troops and find both the time and privacy to focus upon the context in which you've worked your present business plan. To rethink the opportunities you have in light of technology changes and trends. To ask some of the 100 questions or the more introspective questions you'll find in Chapter 8 of this book—for your crew to help you answer. To create awareness of the five bankruptcies among your crew so that time, money, and energy will not be drained from the organization in fighting one or more crises caused by over-commitment of time or money. To challenge the processes you've used for years to create and ship your product and manage your infrastructure. To grow together as a crew—beginning to

Interrelationships 133

practice the airline craft of crew resource management where the whole is greater than the sum of its parts.

> **Your next move might be to gather the senior troops and find both the time and privacy to focus upon the context in which you've worked your present business plan.**

Well, it's time to turn out the lights, pull the big hanger door closed, and lock up.

We've spent some time together talking flying and business processes. We'll bet you never thought of the two as being so similar before. But they certainly are. The lessons we've learned from our aviation counterparts are strong and viable. There is little room for mistakes up there, but we've learned that problems caught early and corrected will keep us from losing control. And experience is the most important asset we have in detecting those problems. We've explored the resource bankruptcies, as well as tools and insights to avoid them. We examined ourselves and our craft for fitness to fly, and we made judgments about our abilities to control the ship.

The final chapter of this book is for you to use as a special resource for your board and executive staff planning meetings over time, examining your own resources and capacity to deal with issues and crises as a C-level and board-based team. I wish you and your team only the best in making more of a success of your enterprise as a result of deep introspection, appropriate planning and response to challenges that face you now and in the future.

All that's left to say is that none of us ever stop learning, even the old salts. They'll be back in the air tomorrow, and surely we'll find them in the hanger whenever they've got some spare time at the end of a long day. Seek them out. Ask for their insights. Everyone has a great story to tell. And for aviators, the hanger seems the best place to tell them.

But this day is all but over. So I'll pull the hanger doors closed, if you'll turn out the lights…

8

Checklist: Reviewing Your Leadership Strategies and Management Insights

This final chapter is intended to be used as a refresher, a resource for you to use in board meetings and executive planning sessions. Here is a list of the strategies and insights discussed in or quoted from this book, followed by critical questions to induce you and your C-level management to examine your position and agree upon your collective response to challenges—both present and future.

Quoted statements from earlier in this book are presented in italics. This list is offered for C-level executives and their boards to discuss and debate, all toward the goal of agreeing upon the best and most efficient ways to extend your enterprise's runway.

You may elect to check off these paragraphs as you respond to the challenges they present—whether you alone respond or your team completes a discussion of the item. Either way, this chapter may become the basis for your book about yourself, your management style, and your company's culture.

Thinking deeply and responding to these challenging questions effectively may take months and years of discussion and thought. Consider tackling small groups of these issues in a dedicated partition of time during board or executive meetings. Consider planning a management retreat to examine and respond to those issues that represent the greatest challenges or opportunities for your organization.

Challenging Your Thoughts About Your Most Critical Resources

1. *Resource "bankruptcies" are the results of failure to identify and use available resources, and the resulting deep deficit in corporate mobility.* Does this statement resonate with you or members of your senior team? Can you think of areas where your company is particularly weak in identifying and leveraging resources for growth?

2. *Resource bankruptcies usually happen so slowly that those in control don't fully realize that they are losing that control and running out of options—until there are no good options left.* Have you ever experienced such a challenge to your enterprise, where you or your team found yourselves in crisis mode solving a problem that was slow to develop but sudden to appear? What would you do differently today?

3. *Failure to grasp the concepts of efficient resource management results in particularly hard punishment in technology-driven enterprises, because of the speed of innovation.* Does your business rely upon technology to an extraordinary extent to drive development or deploy your product? Are you confident that your organization is adept enough to speed products to market while the technology is still appropriate for the product or service?

4. *Vision is everything. Businesses formed and run without it meander their way through the years, usually as examples of enterprises lost in mediocrity.* Have you developed a crisp, easy to repeat, compelling vision for your enterprise?

5. *Business opportunities that were attractive when conceived may become dead-end opportunities at some point simply because of technological obsolescence.* Are any of your products or services near or at end of life? What is your plan for replacement? Is your company threatened by new technologies for which you have no products in the pipeline?

6. *Companies are more likely to thrive in a growing market than in a declining one. Company life cycles should be viewed in light of industry trends. And investments of time and money should be made with—not counter to—the prevailing winds of technology.* Can you identify any of your products or

Checklist

services that seem to be out of phase with the movement of the marketplace? These aberrations could be based upon technology, physical product size, price, processor speed, cosmetic appeal, or any other market appreciation factor.

7. *The core competency of a company resides in its knowledge of its marketplace and the ability to translate that knowledge into products that fit the market and are well received by customer prospects.* What is your company's core competency? How does this translate to protection of your product or service against the competition?

8. *There are few second chances for a product that is released with problems—without overwhelming financial and public relations cost.* Have you experienced overwhelming product problems after release of a product to the market? How did you react? How should you have reacted? Are you prepared to react more effectively if there is a next time? What can you do to avoid that next time?

9. *Our company management needs to review or create a viable and compelling set of statements laying out our vision, mission, goals, and strategies. We should create and respond to vital questions about our position in the global market, our core business, product, corporate structure, people, marketing, and other critical elements of our core structure.* Is this statement true for you and your enterprise? Have you a plan to address this effort?

10. *What would you change if you were a new CEO coming into your enterprise for the first time, with no strings or ties to the past?* Is there any activity you are pursuing that is draining resources that are critical to achieving your goals? Is your staff appropriate for your size and composed mainly of A- and B-grade workers?

11. *Never run out of money. Money represents power and preserves corporate value.* Are you completely aware of your cash burn, cash-out date if appropriate, and have you a plan to address this issue if less than a year in the future?

12. *Many great products or services have been pushed into the market with a great marketing effort and good salespeople evangelizing a new product into a market*

that is just not responsive or ready for the offering. Are you consciously "pushing" products or services into a market that is non-responsive? Or are you focusing on seeding or responding to market demand "pull" and then growing your business to grow that demand? Which methodology is more comfortable to you and your board at this stage of corporate growth?

13. *Human nature dictates that empty space be filled.* Are you guilty of over-expanding your facilities before the need is obvious and compelling?

Thoughts About Use of Money

14. *Never use short-term money to purchase long-term assets.* Have you pursued any opportunities in which you borrowed using working capital assets to finance fixed asset purchases? Are you secure in that decision and aware of the possible consequences?

15. *Have we created a realistic cash flow plan, and do we maintain it regularly?* Do you look at least thirteen weeks ahead in your cash planning? Are there any trends you see that are negative and need attention?

16. *An incremental dollar is worth less right after funding than near the end of the runway. Our actions often reinforce that statement even if our minds reject it.* Is this statement true or false about your behavior with funds invested?

Managing Time and Removing Bottlenecks

17. Do you use a "question chain" in your management decision process, asking "What if…and then what?" before making difficult decisions?

18. *Wasting time is wasting the second most valuable resource you have, other than the cash you raised or borrowed, or earned to grow the business.* Are your C-level executives focused upon maximizing their use of available time to reach your goals? Are any of those executives guilty of

being the bottlenecks that prevent efficient use of other resources within the company? How do you remove those bottlenecks?

19. *People who find themselves approaching time bankruptcy do so because of their own miscalculation; by the conscious or unconscious misappropriation of their own most critical resources.* Have you experienced this phenomenon? If so, what have you done to overcome it?

20. *Good managers of well-run businesses spend no less than 20 percent of the time with their customers, no more than 20 percent on desk work, and at least 10 percent isolated in strategic thinking, undisturbed.* What is your distribution of your time? Is it the most effective use of that time?

21. *Great companies operate with a vision so narrowly focused that most all of us on the outside can explain it with little trouble and in little time.* Is your vision focused well, and can each of your stakeholders explain it and believe in it?

22. Have you identified resources with expertise in areas where you have the most need? Do you feel you have enough expert support?

23. *The conclusion is that quality assurance is always a pay me now or pay me later issue.* Do you have a quality issue that is damaging your reputation? What aggressive moves have you made to cure this problem that will be perceived by the marketplace as effective and laudable?

24. *Poor planning or poor focus leads the CEO to expect the same speed and quality today that he once achieved with his early entrepreneurial team.* Are you guilty of this expectation? How do you change your culture to recapture the sense of urgency once felt throughout the enterprise?

25. *The issues that lead to time bankruptcy always must be addressed in the early stages. When they become large, they are capable of bringing down even the strongest companies.* Do you have any looming issues that derive from deliberate misuse of critical time resources? How do you effectively address those issues?

26. *Bold action is necessary when faced with life-or-death alternatives in which betting the farm may be necessary for survival. But betting the farm again and again is a sure formula for losing the farm.* What is your C-level management track record in balancing the bold against the reasoned action in response to challenges both large and small? Are you risking more than absolutely necessary in a pattern of overreaction to challenging issues?

27. Are your financial backers' goals aligned with C-level management's goals? Is there an expectation by the financial investors that a "single base hit" is not worth the effort, even at the expense of risking survival of the entity at the endgame? Has your board discussed these expectations to the satisfaction of all members?

28. Are you guilty of not keeping up with the movements within your industry as time progresses? If so, what should you do to catch up and lead?

Developing and Using Relationships

29. Who has defined the modern vision and standards in your industry? Do you understand and buy that vision? Do you believe you offer a more compelling vision than your competitors but have not been able to deliver it effectively outside of your company's walls? If so, why?

30. *The most successful companies have been those where competent relationship partners were recruited to help fill the gaps required in the execution of the vision.* What have you and your team done to recruit world-class relationship partners to your board, advisory board, or employ?

31. *Conversely, an entrepreneur's style of "going it alone" has killed more opportunities in the long run than almost any other force by serving to drive away competent help.* Are you in any way guilty of or perceived by others as a "go it alone" manager, failing to use your relationship resources to their best effectiveness?

32. Building strong relationships relatively quickly in time of need requires relationship insights to know who, what, when, where, and how to find needed resources. Are you in a position to recognize and then recruit such vital relationship resources?

33. The culture of your enterprise is more a reflection of the relationship-building actions of the CEO and senior management than any other single factor. Relationships define the personality and often the success or failure of the enterprise. Have you done everything possible to build the culture you believe best for your company, adding relationships that reinforce that culture?

Understanding the Process of Attaining Your Goals

34. One of the benefits of finding experienced managers is that they know the process of building a company, creating a product or service, and managing through a series of expected and unexpected crises to achieve a goal. Conversely, enthusiasm alone cannot overcome a deficit of process knowledge without cost, either in money or in time. Do you and your subordinates recruit people with experience, able to call upon their past victories and defeats to provide leadership and insight perhaps missing in your own background?

35. At seemingly regular points in a company's growth, a series of predictable crises seem to arise, rotating from financial to organizational to management to product or service-related and back to financial. Do you recognize such a pattern in your business? Can you identify some of the signs of each crisis before it arrives and develop initiatives to reduce the impact of such crises upon the organization?

36. One theory is that it takes up to eighteen months to make a management-level change and bring the replacement fully up to speed. Do you agree with this assessment in the light of your experience? Have you developed contingency plans to absorb workloads of managers beginning to show signs of weakness?

37. Every business has one or many bottlenecks preventing a smooth flow of production and most efficient use of resources. Often, that bottleneck is the boss.

Have you spent time with your senior team discussing your corporate bottlenecks and how to remove them? Are you one of those bottlenecks?

38. Are your corporate and personal goals clear enough that you and your senior management understand the process of attaining them? If not, how do you gain insight into such process creation?

39. *Many times, businesses develop highly convoluted flows and paper trails and compartmentalized operations that not only inhibit the achievement of the goal, but obscure the goal entirely.* Have you examined the process of following a sale from initial contact to final closure? Are there impediments to the process that cause frustration at any level of your organization? How could you deal with these effectively?

40. Do you understand the process needed to launch a new product or service? How to reposition an existing product to extend its life? How to find a strategic partner to help grow the business? If not, who have you identified to help you with this understanding?

41. *Superior companies find extraordinarily fast ways to market with quality products. With today's narrow product windows, slow to market often means missing the window entirely.* Do you consider your team effective in creating an environment that is conducive to rapid deployment of new products and services?

Understanding and Managing the Context in Which We Work

42. *Enthusiasm for application of available technologies alone does not excuse bringing products to market that are not yet appropriate for the marketplace or cost-effective enough to justify their use.* Have you deployed any products into the marketplace that may have been too soon to market given the context of the industry? If so, how did you correct the situation? Would you identify the same problem before launch next time?

43. *The trick is to use the fewest resources possible to discern these forces that frustrate the prevailing market direction, finding niches for products and services*

Checklist   143

that open and close but are often either too small or too quick to appear for the larger market leaders to address. What is your track record in finding and defending niche markets? Do you have the resources to create new markets for your products? Or have you consciously planned to take advantage of market trends with product design and releases?

44. Here are three statements from the book. Do you agree with them? Have you been guilty of defying them? What was the result? What would you do differently?

    Don't be too early to enter a market that does not understand the context of the product or the usefulness of the product itself. The effort defies the benefit gained by first-movers paying the price of paving the way with expenditure of time and money to seed a new market.

    Plan for extra time and cost to adhere to standards, regulations, position against competitors, and to educate the market.

    Take advantage of the excitement generated by the press, industry buzz, and new technology breakthroughs that create standard platforms upon which to host your product or service.

45. *Choosing to do nothing in the face of obvious signs of difficulty is an option, but perhaps the least likely option for success. There are always clues to guide you, some from your past experience, and some from past formal education or training.* Have you been guilty of doing nothing or moving too slowly when faced with signs of product failure in the market? What would you do today that you did not do then? Do you believe you would recognize the symptoms of such difficulty earlier today?

46. *Could we become so conservative that our competition's moves will force us to forgo development of a project, lower prices without a clear picture of relative product strengths, or even abandon a niche market entirely because the big players are hyperactive?* Do you have effective knowledge of your resources to fight the competitive battle?

47. Have you become so embroiled in the day-to-day management of your business that you have lost some or most of the context sensitivity you had when you started? Do you have an uncanny knowledge of your competitor's position and the market's condition? Have you been out with your customers and prospects enough to know the coming challenges to your company and your product?

48. *Working from old data or failing to obtain direct, continuous, frequent feedback from customers is a recipe for eventual failure, as the target market moves away from your center of focus.* How recent is your market data? What are you doing to keep it current and make decisions based upon reliable data?

49. *All companies undergo a predictable series of reorganizations or crises that come in cycles during their growth stages. Often, these are brought about by the late recognition that the context has shifted while the company has not.* Can you identify any such crises in your past that came as a result of not recognizing shifts in industry context, trends, and development? Are you and your senior executives better prepared to identify context crises in the future?

Interrelationships Between Forms of Resources

50. Externally induced events can arise at any time, distracting management from directing the resources at hand toward achievement of the corporate goals. Can you identify any time in the past where you have been distracted by external events that were not relevant to the core of your company but caused you to waste cycles or resources pursuing the distraction?

51. *Having a crisis plan that has been developed by your company to cover at least the first steps in crisis response coordination would go a very long way toward focusing the crew during the most critical first hours or days following an externally induced crisis.* Have you discussed and created such a crisis plan covering operations, technology backup, leadership flexibility, and cash availability?

Checklist 145

52. *The more you share the responsibility between you and your cockpit crew, the more likely you are to receive critical feedback and useful contribution by the crew.* Are you effective at delegating tasks, dolling out both responsibility and authority? Have you been accused of micromanagement? Do you see any signs of lack of engagement in the management process by your subordinates during one-on-one and management meetings? Are you responsible for not giving resources and authority to your next level of management?

53. *The insertion of a temporary or permanent change at the executive level will alter the interaction between all of the senior crew members. Until all are quite satisfied that the captain's actions match his or her words, the crew will not work together as a unit to the maximum efficiency level it could achieve.* Have you experienced such a culture shift at the senior levels of your organization because of an executive management change? Did you have to rebuild the confidence of the team? Are you effective at integrating new managers into the organization while preserving the corporate culture?

54. Are you a member of any C-level roundtables or networking organizations that permit open and lengthy discourse among your peers? Who do you turn to when you need advice about management issues?

55. Did this book stimulate you to think in more creative ways about your personal management style and abilities, about your enterprise resources, about positioning in the market, and about planning for your future?

ABOUT THE AUTHOR

Founder and president of Berkus Technology Ventures LLC, Dave Berkus is an early-stage venture capitalist with a hands-on background in technology-based businesses. He has been called one of the most active angels in the nation, with over sixty-five companies receiving his personal investment of time and money over the years. An entrepreneur himself for over fifty years, he has formed and managed successful businesses in the entertainment and software arenas, and has become known as a respected technology industry leader and spokesperson.

Listed in Marquis's *Who's Who in America* and *Who's Who in the World*, Mr. Berkus is current or recent board chairman or board member for numerous public and private Internet- and software-based companies. In recognition of his accomplishments serving as board member or chairman of twenty-four such companies over the years, he was named "Director of the Year—Early-Stage Businesses" by the Forum for Corporate Directors of Orange County, California. In the investment community, he is the managing partner of Berkus Technology Ventures LLC and Kodiak Ventures LP, both seed capital investment funds, and past chairman of the Tech Coast Angels, one of the county's largest groups of early-stage venture investors.

As founder of Computerized Lodging Systems Inc., Mr. Berkus was an early pioneer in the mini-computer industry, innovating numerous technology firsts and guiding Computerized Lodging Systems through a decade of spectacular growth, including two consecutive years on the Inc. 500 list of America's fastest-growing companies. For his accomplishments in advancing technology in the hospitality industry, he was inducted into the Hospitality (HFTP) *International Hall of Fame*, one of only twenty-six so honored worldwide over the years.

Mr. Berkus serves as vice president of marketing for the western region of Boy Scouts of America and is chairman of the advisory board of ABL Organization, a networking organization of CEOs in high-tech businesses.

A graduate of Occidental College, Mr. Berkus currently serves as a trustee of the college. He is a commercial pilot with instrument and multi-engine ratings, and has several times earned Flight Safety International's coveted "Pro Card" for airline transport pilot proficiency.